AMERICA'S
BEST BREAKFASTS

PANCAKE
HOUSE

AMERICA'S
BEST BREAKFASTS

FAVORITE LOCAL RECIPES
from COAST TO COAST

LEE BRIAN SCHRAGER .... *and*
ADEENA SUSSMAN

Photographs by Evan Sung

CLARKSON POTTER/PUBLISHERS

NEW YORK

Published in the United States by Clarkson
Potter/Publishers, an imprint of the Crown
Publishing Group, a division of Penguin Random
House LLC, New York.

www.crownpublishing.com
www.clarksonpotter.com

CLARKSON POTTER is a trademark and
POTTER with colophon is a registered
trademark of Penguin Random House LLC.

Additional photographs by Daniel Johnson
(pages 67 and 71), Alistair Tutton (pages 72 and
105 [Happy Gillis]), and Jennifer Silverberg
(page 105, Goody Goody).

Stock photographs by Shutterstock: © Triff
(pages 7 and 8 [wood texture]) and © Daniela
Pelazza (page 8 [vintage plate]).

Library of Congress Cataloging-in-Publication
Data is available upon request.

ISBN 978-0-553-44721-7
eBook ISBN 978-0-553-44722-4

Printed in China

Book design by Danielle Deschenes
Jacket design by Danielle Deschenes
Jacket photography by Evan Sung

10 9 8 7 6 5 4 3 2 1

First Edition

FOR RR AND THE BROWNS,
MY FAVORITE DINING COMPANIONS
FOR EVERY MEAL OF THE DAY.

CONTENTS

INTRODUCTION 11

THE WEST COAST
and **PACIFIC NORTHWEST** 13

THE MIDWEST 63   THE SOUTH 107

THE NORTHEAST
and
MID-ATLANTIC
.................................177

**SUNDAY,
BLOODY SUNDAY**
.... 228

*How to Get
Perfect Eggs
Every Time*
.... 230

ACKNOWLEDGMENTS......... 234
INDEX 236

THE BREAKFAST TRAIL

THE WEST COAST
AND PACIFIC NORTHWEST

1 LOS ANGELES, CA
Café Gratitude
Connie and Ted's
Pizzeria Mozza
AOC

2 SAN FRANCISCO, CA
Boulettes Larder
Plow
Tartine
San Jalisco
Home of Chef Charles Phan
Foreign Cinema

3 PORTLAND, OR
Fried Egg I'm in Love
Tasty n Sons
Imperial
Sunshine Tavern

4 HONOLULU, HI
Koko Head Cafe

THE MIDWEST

5 OMAHA, NE
Over Easy
Petrow's

6 KANSAS CITY, MO
Bluestem

7 ST. LOUIS, MO
Prasino
Half & Half

8 CLEVELAND, OH
Flying Fig
Lucky's Cafe
Jack Flaps

9 CHICAGO, IL
Ann Sather
Little Goat Diner
Uncle Mike's Place
Mindy's Hot Chocolate
Perennial Virant

THE SOUTH

10 RALEIGH, NC
Joule

11 CHARLESTON, SC
Hominy Grill

12 MEMPHIS, TN
Elwood's Shack

13 BIRMINGHAM, AL
Alabama Biscuit Co.

14 OXFORD, MS
Honey Bee Bakery
Big Bad Breakfast

15 NEW ORLEANS, LA
Li'l Dizzy's
The Old Coffeepot
Dong Phuong

16 HOUSTON, TX
Blacksmith

17 SAN ANTONIO, TX
El Milagrito Cafe

18 AUSTIN, TX
TacoDeli
Lambert's

19 MIAMI, FL
Home of Lee Schrager
Foar
Versailles
Buena Vista Deli
Panther Coffee and Cindy
Kruse's Baked Goods
Eating House
27 Restaurant
Home of Chef Ingrid
Hoffman

THE NORTHEAST
AND MID-ATLANTIC

20 CAMBRIDGE, MA
Sofra

21 NEW YORK, NY
Russ & Daughters Cafe
Barbounia
Home of Chef
Georgette Farkas
Num Pang Nomad
Miss Lily's
Home of Debi Mazar and
Gabriele Corcos

22 PHILADELPHIA, PA
Federal Donuts
Café Lift
High Street on Market

23 BALTIMORE, MD
Maggie's Farm
Blue Moon Cafe
Gertrude's

24 RICHMOND, VA
Millie's
Heritage

25 WASHINGTON, DC
Kapnos
Jaleo
Birch & Barley

INTRODUCTION

RISE AND DINE! When we began thinking about the follow-up to our last book, *Fried & True*, we knew finding a subject with the universal appeal of fried chicken would be a challenge. A few things were clear: Whatever we chose needed to reflect the diversity of cooking in this country today. It would have to provide endless opportunities for downright delicious meals. And it needed to be loved by the masses; after all, who likes cooking in an echo chamber? That's how we arrived at breakfast. To our mind, it's the only one of our traditional "three squares" that's as irresistible in its traditional morning timeslot as it is appropriated for lunch, dinner—or any hour in between.

Really, who *doesn't* have a favorite breakfast dish? The fact that it can often be made using kitchen staples—and that it's the only meal you can get away with eating wearing a bathrobe absolutely guilt-free—only increases its appeal in our eyes. As the first meal of the day, it sets the tone for what lies ahead, a sort of morning manifest destiny with a healthy side of optimism. Sweet or savory? Quick or creative? American or international? The choices are truly limitless.

The best part of our fried chicken adventure was being on the road meeting the greatest cooks in the country, so this time around we built our book out of a series of epic, food-feasting road trips. For the better part of a year we researched, traveled, tasted, and photographed as many spectacular dishes as we could find from coast to coast. That meant weeks traversing the South, Midwest, West Coast, Pacific Northwest, and mid-Atlantic—not to mention our hometowns of New York and Miami, where we leaned heavily on personal favorites (and recommendations from chef friends and local insiders) for inspiration.

Though many of the recipes here are for American-style breakfasts—pancakes, waffles, and biscuits will always have a special place in our hearts—a good number belong to cultures that contribute to our nation's culinary melting pot. From shakshuka to pho, congee to croque monsieur—they're all here, ready for you to try. So sit down, grab your skillet, and get cooking. We hope you enjoy this book as much as we enjoyed putting it together, one delicious bite at a time.

TOP: Lee and Adeena at one of their many meals

BOTTOM: The Bacon Cheddar Potato pancakes (page 91) at Ann Sather in Chicago

CHAPTER ONE

THE

WEST COAST
and
PACIFIC NORTHWEST

═══ LOS ANGELES, CA ═══

CAFÉ GRATITUDE
GOLDEN TURMERIC ICED LATTE............16

CONNIE AND TED'S
LOBSTER SCRAMBLED EGGS.................19

PIZZERIA MOZZA
BREAKFAST PIZZA.........................20

AOC
OVEN-BAKED EGGS WITH WHITE BEANS,
ROASTED TOMATOES, AND OLIVES.......24

═══ SAN FRANCISCO, CA ═══

BOULETTES LARDER
HUBBARD SQUASH PUREE AND SOFT-
SCRAMBLED EGGS.........................29

PLOW
AVOCADO TOAST WITH PICKLED RED
ONIONS AND POACHED EGGS..............30

TARTINE
CROQUE MONSIEUR SANDWICHES........33

SAN JALISCO
POZOLE 37

**HOME OF CHEF CHARLES PHAN OF THE SLANTED
DOOR**
CHÁO (VIETNAMESE CHICKEN AND RICE
PORRIDGE) 38

FOREIGN CINEMA
FRUIT TART "POP TARTS".................43

═══ PORTLAND, OR ═══

FRIED EGG I'M IN LOVE
THE YOLKO ONO SANDWICH 46

TASTY N SONS
CHOCOLATE DOUGHNUTS AND CRÈME
ANGLAISE 49

IMPERIAL
CARAMELIZED GRAPEFRUIT WITH BASIL
SUGAR 53

SUNSHINE TAVERN
KIMCHI PANCAKES 54

═══ HONOLULU, HI ═══

KOKO HEAD CAFE
KOKO MOCO 57

BEST OF THE WEST

Touching down on the West Coast, we knew to expect one thing: the freshest ingredients, put to use in ways that would surprise, satisfy, and inspire. Our expectations were met—and exceeded—every stop along the way, beginning in Los Angeles, where a cool—but never cooler-than-thou—vibe ruled. From the hippie-chic offerings at Café Gratitude in Venice, where the blissed-out clientele served as the restaurant's most ringing endorsement, to the whole-some avocado toast at Plow, we couldn't help but feel more relaxed after just a couple of sun-filled mornings.

Chef friends like Suzanne Goin, an expert practitioner of LA goodness, treated us to dish after dish that reminded us just how fresh and fulfilling breakfast can be. Up north, San Francisco lived up to its reputation as a dining destination equally influenced by its passion for hyper-locavorism and its exceedingly international citizenry. Produce sorcerer Amaryll Schwertner's colorful, thoughtful creations set the tone for a trip filled with great meals that included a visit to Vietnamese chef Charles Phan's home, where he taught us how to make authentic breakfast porridge that blew us away (see page 38). And Portland welcomed us with open arms, with breakfasts that were as comforting as they were thought-provoking. A chocolate doughnut whose main ingredient is mashed potatoes (see page 49)? A pancake packed with fiery kimchi (see page 54)? A broiled grapefruit gilded with emerald-green, basil-infused sugar (see page 53)? Yes, yes, and yes again.

GOLDEN TURMERIC ICED LATTE *...Serves 1*

Imagine a restaurant that's both completely otherworldly and entirely LA, and you've nailed the vibe at Café Gratitude in Venice Beach. Everyone seems a little more Zen here, from the servers and patrons to the dogs leashed on the curb. But really, what else would you expect from an establishment whose co-owner, Ryland Engelhart, calls himself the Chief Inspiration Officer? Even the plates encourage positivity, emblazoned with questions like, "What are you grateful for?" Los Angeles is also the locus of juicing culture; if you've never had an iced latte made with fresh turmeric juice, you may be surprised by how much you love it. It encapsulates a sunny SoCal beach day in a glass: the dusky, earthy flavor of the fresh turmeric, sweetened with honey and enriched with almond milk, is a revelation.

Steam the almond milk, or heat it gently in a small saucepan. Whisk in the honey to dissolve, and let the mixture cool slightly. Fill a tall glass with ice, add the turmeric juice, and top with the almond milk.

1 cup unsweetened, very lightly sweetened, or vanilla **almond milk**

1 tablespoon **honey** or agave

2 tablespoons **fresh turmeric juice**, juiced from 4 ounces fresh turmeric root

COOK'S NOTE

Fresh turmeric is increasingly available at health food stores and upscale supermarkets. If you don't have a juicer, peel the turmeric and process in the small bowl of a food processor or a spice grinder. Place the pulp in a double layer of cheesecloth and squeeze the fresh juice into a bowl; discard the solids. Fresh turmeric juice can be replaced with ¾ teaspoon turmeric powder dissolved in 2 tablespoons water.

OPPOSITE, TOP LEFT: Sunny breakfasts include dishes like chia seed pudding and dairy-free matcha lattes

LOBSTER SCRAMBLED EGGS .... *Serves 4*

Few things are as delicious as soft-scrambled eggs, but this New England–style seafood house—incongruously set in West Hollywood—ups the ante by topping the eggs with lobster and enriching them with melted butter. The chefs cook the lobsters in-house, adding the cooked tomalley—the tasty green stuff you find in the lobster cavity—for extra luxury and flavor. In this recipe, we forgo the home-steamed crustacean for your convenience, but if you have a good fishmonger, ask him to save you some tomalley for this dish.

¾ pound good-quality picked
  lobster meat
8 tablespoons (1 stick) **unsalted
  butter,** melted
12 large **eggs**
½ teaspoon **sea salt**
¼ cup **crème fraîche**
Lobster tomalley from 2 lobsters
  (optional; see headnote)
1 large **lemon,** for zesting
2 tablespoons chopped **fresh chives,**
  plus more for garnish
Pinch of **espelette pepper**
  (see Cook's Note, page 30)
  or paprika (optional), for garnish
Buttered toast or grilled bread,
  for serving

1 In a small saucepan, gently warm the lobster meat and butter over the lowest heat (lobster will overcook if the flame is too high), 2 to 3 minutes. Remove from the heat and keep warm. In a mixing bowl, whisk the eggs and season with the salt.

2 Heat 1 tablespoon of the warmed butter from the lobster in a slope-sided nonstick skillet over medium-low heat. Add the eggs and gently cook, whisking constantly, until they slowly start congealing into what looks like small, cottage cheese curds, 15 minutes. Whisk in the crème fraîche and, if using, the lobster tomalley; the texture of the eggs will become a bit looser. Cook until the eggs tighten up slightly, 1 to 2 minutes. Using a Microplane, grate the lemon zest directly into the eggs, then stir in the chives, reserving some of the zest and chives for garnish. Remove the skillet from the heat.

3 Remove the lobster from the butter and divide it among 4 serving bowls, saving the prettiest and most vibrantly colored pieces of meat for the top. Spoon the eggs over the lobster, garnish with the reserved lobster pieces, the rest of the chives, a pinch of espelette, and the rest of the lemon zest. Serve with toast.

BREAKFAST PIZZA .... *Serves 3*

Securing a seat at the counter at Nancy Silverton's pizza palace is a challenge, and for good reason. Pies, made to order, come out of the smoldering oven supported by the most masterful crust we've seen: pliant, puffy, crisp-edged, and slightly doughy—everything you could want and more. The revelation of breakfast pizza, which Silverton unearthed from her recipe archive for us, was the *panna*—salted whipped cream used to prime the dough's surface before topping it with a flurry of cheeses, meats, and potatoes. The instructions may seem exacting, but following them to a T will make you the most experienced pizzaiolo for miles around. Of course, store-bought pizza dough is an option if you're pressed for time or looking for a shortcut when entertaining.

1 Whip the cream and salt in a stand mixer, or with a hand mixer, on medium speed until it reaches soft peaks just stiff enough to spread. Refrigerate until ready to use.

2 Remove the racks from the oven and place a pizza stone or a heavy duty baking sheet, underside facing up, on the oven floor. Preheat the oven and stone to 500°F for at least 1 hour. Dust a pizza peel with semolina or cover with a 10 × 10-inch piece of parchment paper. (If you don't have a peel, use a flat cookie sheet.)

3 Place 1 round of dough on a generously floured work surface and dust it lightly with flour. Using your fingertips as though you were tapping on piano keys, gently tap the center of the dough to flatten it slightly, leaving a 1-inch rim untouched. Pick up the dough, ball both your fists, and with your fists facing your body, place the top edge of the dough

recipe continues

½ cup **heavy cream**
⅛ teaspoon **kosher salt**

Semolina or cornmeal, for dusting the pizza peel (optional)
Pizza Dough (recipe follows)
All-purpose flour, for dusting the work surface
3 tablespoons **extra-virgin olive oil**
Kosher salt
6 ounces **low-moisture mozzarella,** cut into ½-inch cubes (1½ cups)
9 ounces **Sottocenere al tartufo or other truffle cheese,** shredded
3 ounces **Fontina,** cut into ½-inch cubes (¾ cup)
12 **scallions,** white and green parts included, thinly sliced on an extreme bias
3 small **Yukon Gold potatoes,** steamed, cooled, peeled, and cut into ¼-inch-thick rounds
6 thick slices **applewood-smoked bacon**
2 tablespoons **fresh thyme leaves**
3 large **eggs**
Maldon or other flaky sea salt, such as fleur de sel

Roma-Grosseto

1	Ⓐ	2	†	✕	Ⓐ		✕	✕
30036	3106	1662	3028	3032				3254
E2	R2	E2	R2					
Ⓟ	🚲♿	Ⓟ	⚲					

venienza	ME							
ni								
na								
lana	I							
se	3.56							
vere	I							
o								
egene								
-Palidoro								
veteri								
veteri								
a								
astro								
Arger								
ale								
inazioi								
1, il 6/1								
ma								
Piombino	5.2							
ma	a.	5.47	6.44	7.0				
Destinazione			PI					

no subire modifiche. 2 Si effettua nei giorni lavor
bato e nei giorni festivi fino al 5/4, il sabato dall'11/4 al 30/5: sospeso i 25/4.

on your fists so the round stretches downward against the backs of your hands, away from them. Move the circle of dough around your fists like the hands of a clock so the dough continues to stretch downward into a circle. When the dough has stretched to about 10 inches in diameter, lay it on the prepared peel or baking sheet.

4 Brush the rim of the dough with 1 tablespoon of the olive oil and season the entire surface with kosher salt. Brush the surface with ¼ cup of the whipped panna. Scatter one-third of the cheeses over the surface of the pizza. Scatter one-third of the scallions over the cheeses, arrange one-third of the sliced potatoes on top of the scallions, and sprinkle the potato slices with kosher salt. Cut 2 of the bacon slices in half crosswise and lay 1 piece on each quadrant of the pizza. Sprinkle 1 teaspoon of the thyme leaves over the pizza.

5 Place the pizza in the oven by sliding it with one decisive push from the pizza peel onto the stone (or sliding the pizza from the flat baking sheet onto the preheated baking sheet in the oven.) Bake for 5 minutes, or until the pizza is halfway cooked. Crack 1 egg into a small bowl, remove the pizza from the oven, and slide the egg onto the center of the pizza. Return the pizza to the oven until the crust is golden brown and the yolk is still slightly runny, 5 to 6 minutes.

6 Remove the pizza from the oven and cut it into quarters, stopping at the edge of the egg so it stays intact, and making sure that each slice of pizza gets a piece of bacon. Sprinkle the egg with the sea salt, sprinkle ½ teaspoon thyme leaves over the pizza, and serve immediately. Repeat the process with the remaining 2 dough balls.

TOP TO BOTTOM: Shaping the dough and adding the toppings

PIZZA DOUGH .... *Makes 6 balls of dough*

1 Pour 1 cup of the water into the bowl of a stand mixer. Add the yeast and let the mixture activate for 5 to 8 minutes. Add 1¼ cups of the bread flour, the rye flour, and the wheat germ, and stir with a wooden spoon until combined. Wrap the bowl in plastic wrap and seal with another piece for an airtight seal. Let the dough rest at room temperature for 1½ hours.

2 Uncover the bowl and add the remaining water, bread flour, and the honey. Fit the mixer with a dough hook and mix on low speed for 2 minutes. Add the salt and mix on medium speed until the dough starts to pull away from the sides of the bowl, 6 to 7 minutes (if the dough is too sticky and does not pull away from the sides at all, throw a small handful of flour into the bowl). While the dough is mixing, lightly grease a bowl large enough to hold the dough when it doubles in size. Turn the dough out into the oiled bowl; wrap the bowl with plastic wrap, using the same method as before; and rest at room temperature for 45 minutes.

3 Dust your work surface lightly with flour and turn the dough out onto the floured surface. Acting as if the round has 4 sides, fold the edges of the dough toward the center. Turn the dough over and return it, folded side down, to the bowl. Cover the bowl again with plastic wrap and set it aside for 45 minutes.

4 Dust your work surface again lightly with flour and turn the dough out onto the surface. Divide it into 6 equal parts. Tuck the edges of each dough round under itself. Cover the rounds with a clean dish towel and let them rest for 5 minutes. With lightly floured hands, gather each round into a taut ball.

5 Dust a baking sheet generously with flour and place the dough rounds on it. Cover with the dish towel and let the dough proof at room temperature for 1 hour. The dough is best when made into pizzas the same day.

1½ cups **warm tap water**
1½ teaspoons **compressed yeast,** or ½ teaspoon active dry yeast
2½ cups plus 2 tablespoons **unbleached bread flour,** plus more as needed
1½ teaspoons **dark or medium rye flour** (optional)
1 teaspoon **wheat germ**
1 teaspoon **mild honey,** such as clover or wildflower
1½ teaspoons **kosher salt**
1 tablespoon **olive oil,** for greasing the bowl

Chef Nancy Silverton of Pizzeria Mozza

OVEN-BAKED EGGS
WITH WHITE BEANS, ROASTED TOMATOES, AND OLIVES

··· *Serves 4*

LA chef Suzanne Goin has had one version or another of oven-baked eggs on the brunch menu at her restaurants The Larder and AOC for as long as she can remember. In this version, the white beans, roasted tomatoes, and cavolo nero (a southern Italian green similar to dinosaur kale) braise together and the eggs, placed on top, cook right into that rustic stew. The tomatoes release their juices, and the eggs soak into the beans and still get nice color and texture on top. A final sprinkling of lemony gremolata over the top lends a bit of brightness and just enough acidity.

For the Beans

1 cup **small dried white beans**

¼ cup **extra-virgin olive oil**

1 large sprig **fresh rosemary**

1 dried **chile de árbol,** crumbled

1 medium **onion,** diced

1 medium **fennel bulb,** trimmed
   and diced (1 cup)

6 **garlic cloves,** smashed

2 tablespoons **fresh thyme leaves**

1 **bay leaf**

1 tablespoon **kosher salt**

For the Cavolo Nero

Kosher salt

3 bunches of **cavolo nero** or dinosaur kale,
   center ribs removed

¼ cup **extra-virgin olive oil**

1 small sprig of **fresh rosemary**

recipe continues

1 _**Make the beans:**_ Put the beans in a medium bowl, cover with 4 inches of cold water, and soak overnight; drain and rinse. Heat a medium saucepan over high heat for 2 minutes. Pour in the olive oil, add the rosemary sprig and crumbled chile, and let them sizzle in the oil for 1 minute. Add the onion, fennel, garlic, thyme, and bay leaf and cook, stirring, until the onion is softened, 1 to 2 minutes.

2 Add the white beans and cook, stirring to coat the beans in the oil, for 2 minutes. Cover with water by 3 inches, raise the heat, and bring to a boil. Reduce the heat to low and press a paper towel over the beans to keep them under the surface. Simmer for 30 minutes, add the salt, and continue cooking until the beans are tender, 1 hour, adding water if necessary. Remove the beans from the heat, discard the paper towel, and allow them to cool in their liquid.

3 _**Make the cavolo nero:**_ Prepare an ice water bath in a large bowl. Bring a large pot of heavily salted water to a boil over high heat. Working in batches, blanch the cavolo nero for 2 minutes, submerge in the ice water bath, drain, let cool, and squeeze out the excess water with your hands.

4 Heat a large pot or Dutch oven over medium heat for 2 minutes. Pour in 2 tablespoons of the olive oil, add the rosemary sprig and crumbled chile, and let them sizzle in the oil for 1 minute. Reduce the heat to medium-low, add the sliced onion, and season with 1/2 teaspoon of salt and the pepper. Cook for 2 minutes, then stir in the sliced garlic and continue to cook, stirring often with a wooden spoon, until the onion is soft and starts to brown, 5 to 7 minutes.

1 dried **chile de árbol**
1 medium **onion**, sliced (1 cup)
Pinch of **freshly ground black pepper**
2 **garlic cloves**, thinly sliced

For the Roasted Tomatoes

4 **plum (Roma) tomatoes**, halved lengthwise
2 tablespoons **olive oil**
1/4 teaspoon **kosher salt**
1/4 teaspoon **freshly ground black pepper**

For the Gremolata

2 tablespoons finely chopped **fresh flat-leaf parsley**
1/2 teaspoon finely grated **lemon zest**
1/2 teaspoon minced **garlic**

For the Baked Eggs

1/4 cup **oil-cured Moroccan-style black olives**, pitted and sliced
8 large **eggs**
Kosher salt and **freshly ground black pepper**

COOK'S NOTES

Be sure to start this recipe the day before by soaking the beans. Beans can be made up to 3 days in advance and stored in the refrigerator.

5 Add the cavolo nero and remaining 2 tablespoons olive oil, stirring to coat the greens with oil and onions. Season with ¼ teaspoon salt and cook slowly over low heat, stirring often, until the greens turn dark, almost black, and get slightly crispy on the edges, 30 minutes. Remove and discard the rosemary and the chile.

6 Meanwhile, ***roast the tomatoes:*** Preheat the oven to 450°F. Place the tomatoes on a small baking sheet, drizzle with the olive oil, and season with the salt and pepper. Roast until the tomatoes begin to break apart and char, 30 minutes.

7 ***Make the gremolata:*** Chop the parsley, lemon zest, and garlic together until very finely minced; set aside.

8 ***Bake the eggs:*** Raise the oven temperature to 500°F. Place the beans, along with 1 cup of their cooking liquid, in a large (at least 12-inch) cast-iron skillet. Place the cavolo nero on top of the beans, then cover with the tomatoes and the olives. Roast until the beans and vegetables are thoroughly heated, 8 to 10 minutes. Carefully remove the skillet from the oven, crack in the eggs, and season with salt and pepper to taste. Return to the oven and bake until the eggs are just set, 4 to 5 minutes. Remove from the oven, divide among shallow bowls, and sprinkle with the gremolata.

TOP: Fried chicken and waffles, another of Goin's breakfast classics

BOTTOM: Chef Suzanne Goin

HUBBARD SQUASH PUREE
AND SOFT-SCRAMBLED EGGS..*Serves 4*

In a quiet corner of the Ferry Plaza Farmers Market, Chef Amaryll Schwertner has created a temple to the kind of seasonal, local, produce-heavy cuisine the Bay Area has become famous for. Often monochromatic and always delicious, Schwertner's food—from a cheese plate that is a study in white to this gorgeous plate of slow-cooked squash and soft-scrambled eggs—simplifies ingredients down to their most basic form of deliciousness. It doesn't hurt that the restaurant—decorated in muted tones of white and wood and accented with dramatic displays of fruits and vegetables—overlooks the glittering San Francisco Bay.

3 pounds **Hubbard or other orange winter squash,** peeled, seeded, and cut into 1-inch cubes (8 cups)

½ teaspoon **sea salt,** plus more for garnish

1 tablespoon **unsalted butter,** plus more for scrambling the eggs

1 tablespoon **fresh lemon juice**

8 large **eggs**

Extra-virgin olive oil, for drizzling

½ cup finely grated **Parmigiano-Reggiano cheese**

1　In a heavy-bottomed saucepan, combine the squash with ½ cup water and add ¼ teaspoon of the salt. Press parchment paper onto the surface of the squash, set the saucepan over low heat, and cook for 2 hours, until the squash is a soft puree, stirring and checking every 20 minutes to ensure that there is still some water in the pan, and adding water 2 tablespoons at a time if necessary.

2　Cool slightly, then pass the squash through a fine-mesh strainer into a bowl, discarding the solids (or puree in a food processor until smooth). Stir in the butter, lemon juice, and remaining ¼ teaspoon salt.

3　During the last 15 minutes of cooking the squash, soft-scramble the eggs (see page 231). Mound the squash puree among 4 rimmed plates, then top with the eggs. Drizzle with olive oil, season with salt to taste, and sprinkle with the cheese.

CLOCKWISE FROM TOP LEFT: The iconic Ferry Building clock, Chef Amaryll Schwertner, soft-scrambled eggs served with the shell on the plate

AVOCADO TOAST
WITH PICKLED RED ONIONS AND POACHED EGGS ....*Serves 4*

Avocado toast is a relatively new staple on menus at all the right places, but we can't say we're one bit surprised. Sure, avocadoes are healthy, but a few creamy, rich slices are also just as luxurious as a pat of butter or schmeer of cream cheese. Unlike many versions, Plow's avocado toast recipe doesn't call for mashing the avocado. All of the dishes from husband-and-wife team Joel Bleskacek and Maxine Siu have special flourishes, in this case the dead-simple pickled red onions and a sprinkling of espelette pepper, a mild chile pepper hailing from France's Basque region.

Brush the bread on both sides with olive oil and toast in a griddle or skillet over medium-high heat until golden, 1 to 2 minutes per side. Fan the avocado slices over the bread, then season with salt to taste. For each bread slice, scatter one-quarter of the onions over the avocado. Poach the eggs (see page 231), then gently arrange a poached egg on top of the onions. Sprinkle with a pinch of salt and the espelette pepper.

4 thick slices **country bread**

Extra-virgin olive oil

2 small or 1 large ripe **avocado** (preferably Hass), sliced

Kosher salt to taste

½ cup **Pickled Red Onions** (recipe follows)

4 large **eggs**

Pinch of **espelette pepper** (see Cook's Note) or paprika

--- **COOK'S NOTE** ---

Espelette is a rare variety of pepper from France. You can order it at www.worldspice.com.

PICKLED RED ONIONS ....*Makes 1 cup*

In a small saucepan, bring the vinegar, ¼ cup water, the bay leaf, chile, sugar, and salt to a boil. Place the onion slices in a nonreactive bowl, pour the hot liquid over them, and let sit for at least 1 hour before serving. After the onions have come to room temperature, chill in the refrigerator if desired. Pickled onions keep, refrigerated, for up to 2 weeks.

¼ cup **Champagne vinegar**

1 **bay leaf**

1 dried **chile de árbol**, broken in half (or 1 dried Thai bird chile)

1½ teaspoons **sugar**

¼ teaspoon **kosher salt**

1 small **red onion**, sliced

CROQUE MONSIEUR SANDWICHES

Serves 4

There are bakers, and then there are baking superstars. Chad Robertson and Liz Prueitt, revolutionaries of American artisan bread, are two of those stars, bakers whose morning buns, croissants, and sandwiches engender passionate followings and massive queues every morning at their Mission District bakery. While we're still weeping over the flakiness of those croissants and morning buns, we were equally smitten with these creamy open-faced sandwiches filled with ham, cheese, and the grassy freshness of asparagus hidden underneath. If you get one at Tartine, it'll be served on a signature slice of bread. But if making at home, take the time—and spend the money—to source the best loaf possible.

1 Preheat the oven to 425°F.

2 **Make the bechamel:** In a heavy saucepan, melt the butter over medium-low heat. Add the flour and whisk until the mixture bubbles slightly, but has not yet begun to brown, 1 minute. Whisk in the nutmeg, bay leaf, and onion and continue cooking until the onion softens and the mixture browns a bit and gives off a slightly nutty aroma, 2 to 3 minutes. Whisk in the milk and bring to a boil; the mixture should thicken immediately. If not, whisk for 1 minute. Season with salt and pepper to taste and remove from the heat.

3 **Make the sandwiches:** In a large bowl, toss the asparagus with the oil. Arrange the bread on a baking sheet and spread each slice with ¼ cup of the bechamel, then top with 1 slice of ham, 4 spears of asparagus, and 2 slices of cheese. Bake, checking after 9 minutes and rotating as needed, until the cheese is golden and bubbling, 12 to 13 minutes.

For the Bechamel

2 tablespoons **unsalted butter**

2 tablespoons **all-purpose flour**

⅛ teaspoon **freshly grated nutmeg**

1 **bay leaf**

½ cup finely chopped **yellow onion**

1¼ cups **whole milk,** warmed

Kosher salt and **freshly ground black pepper**

For the Sandwiches

16 **asparagus spears,** trimmed

1 tablespoon **extra-virgin olive oil**

4 ¾-inch slices **day-old country bread**

4 ⅛-inch slices **smoked ham**

8 slices **Gruyère cheese**

BOTTOM LEFT: Liz Prueitt and Chad Robertson

Craftsman and Wolves

Just a few blocks from Tartine you'll find Craftsman and Wolves, a hipster's bakery fantasy come true. Inside, minimalist design meets maximalist pastries, including a composed topiary-like mound of vacherins and flaky, perfectly square chocolate "croissant stacks" that create pandemonium among locals. But if there's one item the bakery is best known for, it's the Rebel Within—an oozy soft-boiled egg stuffed inside a meaty, cheesy, super-savory muffin named after a country and western song.

Although such an ingenious invention may seem like it was carefully conceived, in fact it was nothing more than a happy accident. One day, pastry chef William Werner accidentally undercooked the yolks in his new invention. Rather than trashing the results, he threw caution to the wind and served them. Needless to say, they were a hit, and there you have the history of a modern San Francisco classic. But there's just one hitch: the proprietary recipe is so top-secret, you'll have to visit San Francisco to try one.

TOP: The Rebel Within harbors a poached egg inside a savory muffin

BOTTOM: Pastry chef William Werner

POZOLE (PORK AND HOMINY STEW) .... *Serves 8 to 10*

If San Jalisco's Pozole feels like your favorite meal at home transported to a restaurant setting, it's no wonder; three generations of the Padilla family have helped build it into a Mission District institution. If you head in on a weekend, you'll find many a sleepy-eyed soul seeking a steaming bowl of this deeply flavorful soup, named for the snowy-white lumps of hominy (an oversized variety of corn) contained within that help make it a hangover cure without compare. "It's great for a big family meal when you want to make something filling, easy, and inexpensive," said Sophia Reyes-Martinez, daughter of owner, Dolores "Josie" Padilla-Reyes. Josie makes the Pozole on Fridays in huge quantities, then waits for the crowds to come.

1   In a 6-quart stockpot heat the oil over medium-high heat. In a bowl toss the pork with the chopped garlic, cumin, oregano, ½ teaspoon salt, and the pepper. Cook the pork, stirring once or twice, until deeply browned, 8 minutes. Add the onion, 1 of the dried chiles, and the head of garlic and cook, stirring occasionally, until the onion starts to soften, 4 more minutes.

2   Add 12 cups of water, bring to a boil, lower the heat, and simmer, occasionally skimming the foam from the top, 1 hour.

3   Once the broth is cooked, in a separate saucepan, bring the tomatoes and remaining dried chile to a boil, reduce the heat, and simmer for 15 minutes. Transfer the tomato mixture to a blender, add the paprika, and blend until smooth. Add the remaining tomatoes to the soup along with the hominy and the tablespoon of salt. Cook for another 30 minutes. Divide among bowls and serve with radishes, cabbage, cilantro, and lime wedges.

3 tablespoons **vegetable oil**

2 pounds **pork butt**, cut into chunks

6 fresh **garlic cloves**, chopped, plus 1 whole **garlic head**, unpeeled

1 tablespoon **cumin**

2 teaspoons **dried oregano**

½ teaspoon plus 1 tablespoon **salt**

½ teaspoon **freshly ground black pepper**

1 jumbo **onion**, quartered

2 dried **California or Anaheim chiles**, divided, or 3 tablespoons chili powder

3 large **tomatoes** (about 1¼ pounds), chopped

2 teaspoons **paprika**

3 15-ounce cans **hominy**, drained and rinsed

For serving

Thinly sliced, fresh radishes
Shredded cabbage
Cilantro sprigs
Lime wedges

CHÁO (VIETNAMESE CHICKEN AND RICE PORRIDGE) .... *Serves 6 to 8*

"Of all the foods I grew up eating in Vietnam, chicken and rice porridge is the thing people always come back to," Charles Phan told us when we visited him at his spacious, art-filled apartment in San Francisco. When he opened the first iteration of his Slanted Door restaurant in 1995, Phan showed Americans just how exciting and varied Vietnamese food can be. At home, you'll often find him making this Vietnamese version of congee, which he calls "the ultimate hangover and flu cure." When we arrived, a chicken was already simmering in a pot of hot water on the stove. Phan uses a special variety of bird, prized for a sinewy leanness that reminds him of chickens back in Vietnam. At your local grocer, look for a younger chicken that weighs no more than four pounds.

1 3½- to 4-pound **chicken**

6 whole **scallions,** plus 6 more, white and light green parts only, thinly sliced, for serving

1 thumb-sized piece of **fresh ginger** (about 3 inches), peeled and crushed, plus a 2-inch piece, peeled and cut into ¼-inch-thick coins

1 tablespoon plus ½ teaspoon **kosher salt,** plus more to taste

1 cup **jasmine rice**

3 quarts good-quality **chicken stock**

8 warm **Chinese Doughnuts** (recipe follows)

2 cups **canola oil**

6 to 8 large **shallots,** thinly sliced (3½ to 4 cups)

½ bunch of fresh **cilantro,** chopped, for serving

8 **lime wedges** (optional), for serving

Freshly ground black pepper

recipe continues

1 **Poach the chicken:** Bring a large pot of water to a boil over high heat. Add the chicken, whole scallions, crushed ginger, and 1 tablespoon salt. Return to a boil and boil for 15 minutes. Turn off the heat, cover the pot, and let stand for 25 minutes.

2 Just before the chicken is ready, prepare a large ice-water bath. When the chicken is done, remove it from the pot and immediately submerge it in the ice water, which will stop the cooking and give the meat a firmer texture. Reserve 2 cups of the chicken cooking water and strain through a fine-mesh strainer; discard the rest or save it to make stock with the skin and bones. Let the chicken remain in the ice bath until it is cool enough to handle, about 20 minutes, then remove from the water and pat dry. Pull the meat from the bones, discarding the bones and skin or reserving them to make stock. Shred the meat with your fingers.

3 **Make the porridge:** Place the rice in a fine-mesh sieve and rinse well under cold running water. In a large pot, combine the rice, stock, ginger, and the 2 cups reserved chicken cooking water. Bring to a boil over high heat, lower the heat to a simmer, and cook, uncovered, for 2 hours. Stir occasionally, especially toward the end, as the rice will have broken down and the mixture will have a porridge-like consistency. Season with 1/2 teaspoon salt.

4 While the rice cooks, you can roll out the dough for the doughnuts and fry them as outlined in the recipe.

5 **Make the shallots:** Heat the oil over medium-high heat until it registers 275°F on a deep-fry thermometer. Add the shallots and cook, stirring, until light brown, 8 minutes. Using a slotted spoon, transfer the shallots to a paper towel-lined plate to drain.

6 Increase the heat to high and place the fried shallots in a metal sieve that can be used to fry them again in the oil. When the oil registers 350°F on the deep-fry thermometer, lower the sieve with the shallots into the oil (in batches if necessary) and cook until just crispy and well browned, 3 to 5 seconds, watching carefully so the shallots don't burn. Transfer to a paper towel-lined plate to drain.

7 To serve, place the sliced scallions, cilantro, lime wedges (if using), fried shallots, and doughnut slices in separate bowls, to be passed around the table. Ladle the porridge into warmed bowls. Top each serving with an equal amount of the shredded chicken and a pinch of pepper.

CHINESE DOUGHNUTS ·················· *Makes 8 doughnuts*

Start this recipe the night before you're planning to serve the doughnuts, as the dough needs to rest in the refrigerator. When making these to serve with cháo, plan to roll and fry the dough after you start the porridge so that the doughnuts are served warm.

1 In a large bowl, whisk together the flour, baking powder, and baking soda. In a small bowl, dissolve the sugar and salt in 1 cup of hot water. Form a well in the center of the dry ingredients and add the egg yolk. Gradually pour the water mixture into the well, whisking to combine with the yolk. Switch to a wooden spoon and continue mixing until the wet and dry ingredients are well combined. The dough will be sticky; if it looks dry, add more water, a tablespoon at a time.

2 Drizzle in the 2 tablespoons canola oil and knead into the dough until smooth, 2 to 3 minutes. Cover the bowl with plastic wrap and let rest at room temperature for 1 hour. Refrigerate overnight.

3 Remove the dough from the refrigerator and allow it to come to room temperature for about 30 minutes. Flour a work surface, your hands, and a rolling pin. Divide the dough in half and transfer one half from the bowl to your work surface, keeping the other half covered in the bowl. Roll the dough into a 6 × 12-inch rectangle about ½ inch thick. Cut eight 1½-inch-wide strips lengthwise, then run a sharp knife down the center of each strip to gently score the dough (do not cut all the way through). Lightly brush the tops of 4 strips with water, then stack the other 4 strips on top, scored sides facing each other, to form doubled stacks. Gently press the top strip on each stack so it adheres to the bottom strip.

recipe continues

3 cups **all-purpose flour,** plus more for dusting the work surface

2 tablespoons **baking powder**

¼ teaspoon **baking soda**

1 tablespoon **sugar**

½ teaspoon **kosher salt**

1 large **egg yolk**

2 tablespoons **canola oil,** plus more for deep-frying

─────── **COOK'S NOTE** ───────

These Chinese-style doughnuts— a fixture at pho restaurants in Vietnam—are surprisingly easy to execute and, along with the shredded chicken, can be made a day ahead.

4 Transfer to a plate so your work surface is clear, then lightly cover with plastic wrap and let rest for 15 minutes. Repeat with the remaining half of the dough. You should have 8 doughnuts.

5 Pour oil to a depth of 2 inches into a wok or large, high-sided pot and heat to 350°F on a deep-frying thermometer. When the oil is ready, carefully add 2 doughnuts and cook, turning them continuously and submerging them beneath the oil until golden brown, 4 to 6 minutes. Using a spider or tongs, transfer the doughnuts to paper towels to drain. Repeat with the remaining 6 doughnuts, allowing the oil to return to temperature before adding each batch. Cut the doughnuts on the diagonal into 2-inch pieces and serve warm.

Freshly fried Chinese doughnuts

FRUIT TART "POP TARTS" .... *Makes 6*

For more than twenty years, Foreign Cinema has been one of San Francisco's most sought-after brunch destinations. Chefs Gayle Pirie and John Clark are talented practitioners of all things seasonal, local, and delicious, one of the prime examples being these flaky pastries filled with whatever fruit is at its peak. The dough is simple to make, and this recipe comes together easily with whatever homemade jams you love to make—or feel free to substitute a good-quality store-bought brand.

1 Preheat the oven to 375°F. Line a cookie sheet with parchment paper.

2 In a food processor, pulse the flour, salt, and granulated sugar until just combined. Add the butter and pulse until the mixture forms pea-sized pieces. Add the egg yolks, one at a time, and pulse until well blended. Gradually sprinkle the water over the mixture and pulse just until any small, irregular clumps are smoothed out. Wrap the dough in plastic wrap and refrigerate until firm, 20 minutes.

3 On a lightly floured surface, roll the dough into a 10 × 18-inch rectangle. Using a pizza cutter or pastry wheel, cut the dough down the center into 2 long strips, then cut each strip into six 3 × 5-inch rectangles, for a total of 12 rectangles, each about the size of a small postcard.

recipe continues

1⅓ cups **all-purpose flour,** plus more for dusting

Pinch of **kosher salt**

2 tablespoons **granulated sugar**

5 tablespoons cold **unsalted butter,** cut into pieces

2 large **egg yolks**

2 tablespoons **cold water**

1 large **egg,** beaten with 1 tablespoon water, for the egg wash

1 cup **seasonal preserves** or jam

Turbinado or raw sugar

Confectioners' sugar

4 Using a pastry scraper, gently place 6 rectangles on the lined cookie sheet. Brush the edges with egg wash and spread 2 tablespoons jam in the center of each rectangle. Arrange the 6 remaining rectangles on top of the jam-filled ones, aligning the corners. Crimp all the edges of the rectangle with a fork to close each tart. (At this point, the tarts can be refrigerated for 1 hour or frozen for 20 minutes.) Pierce the top of each fruit tart with a fork 4 times, then brush the tops with egg wash and sprinkle with turbinado sugar.

5 Bake until the tarts are golden brown, 20 to 25 minutes. Cool on the baking sheet slightly, then sprinkle with confectioners' sugar.

THE YOLKO ONO SANDWICH .... *Serves 4*

Portland's a food truck sort of town, and Fried Egg I'm in Love is the embodiment of the genre: creative, quirky, and downright delicious. Jace Krause and his friend and bandmate Ryan Lynch, both relative newcomers to the town, were looking for a way to harness their love of breakfast—and supplement their income between gigs. Inspired by the fluffy scrambled eggs Krause's grandmother made when he was a child, they decided to make eggs the focal point of their truck. "What's better than a fried egg?" asked Krause as he cracked eggs onto the grill of the compact cart, housed right next to a mobile home–cum–hair salon that shares their tiny asphalt lot. All of the sandwiches have quirky music-inspired names—Sriracha Mix-A-Lot, Egg Zeppelin, 'Rito Suave, to name a few—and delicious touches, such as house-made pesto. Making breakfast sausage is a worthwhile endeavor, but if you're pressed for time, a good-quality store-bought kind will do the trick.

1 **Make the sausage:** In the small bowl of a food processor, pulse the onion, mustard, garlic, paprika, oregano, salt, and pepper until the mixture is very fine and orange in color. In a large bowl, combine the pork with the onion puree and mix thoroughly. Divide into 4 equal balls, and roll until compact.

2 **Make the sandwiches:** Preheat a griddle or large cast-iron skillet over medium-low heat. Butter one side of each slice of bread, then spread the other side of each slice with 1½ tablespoons pesto and sprinkle with 1 tablespoon cheese. Grill 4 slices of bread, buttered side down, until golden, about 2 minutes; set aside. Repeat with the remaining 4 slices of bread.

recipe continues

For the Sausage Patties
(see Cook's Note)

1 cup roughly chopped **yellow onion**

1 teaspoon **yellow mustard**

1 teaspoon minced **garlic**

½ teaspoon **paprika**

½ teaspoon **dried oregano**

½ teaspoon **kosher salt**

¼ teaspoon **freshly ground black pepper**

1 pound **ground pork** or loose pork sausage meat

For the Sandwiches

2 to 3 tablespoons **unsalted butter,** melted

8 slices **sourdough bread**

¾ cup **Pesto** (recipe follows)

½ cup finely grated **Parmigiano-Reggiano cheese**

1 tablespoon **vegetable oil**

4 large **eggs**

Freshly ground black pepper to taste

Cayenne pepper to taste

————— **COOK'S NOTE** —————

Store-bought sausage patties can be substituted for the homemade sausage. You can also make individual uncooked sausage patties ahead of time and freeze them, tightly sealed in plastic wrap, for up to 3 months.

3 Raise the heat to medium-high. Place the sausage balls on the griddle and press into patties slightly larger than the bread (patties will shrink during cooking). Cook until the edges are charred, 4 to 5 minutes per side. Set a sausage patty on top of 4 of the grilled bread slices. Wipe the griddle clean and add the oil. Crack the eggs into the pan and cook, sunny-side up (see page 233). Place an egg on each sausage patty, then top with the other slice of grilled bread. Season with pepper and cayenne to taste.

Jace Krause (left) and Brian Lynch

PESTO .... *Makes 1½ cups*

3 cups lightly packed **fresh basil leaves**
⅔ cup shredded **Parmigiano-Reggiano cheese**
¼ cup **pine nuts**
⅔ cup **olive oil,** plus more if necessary
1½ tablespoons minced **garlic**
Salt and **freshly ground black pepper** to taste

In the small bowl of a food processor, pulse all ingredients until just incorporated, 10 to 15 pulses. Scrape down the sides of the bowl, then process until you get a spreadable texture, an additional 30 to 45 seconds (add additional oil if necessary). Season with salt and pepper to taste.

CHOCOLATE DOUGHNUTS AND CRÈME ANGLAISE..... *Serves 6*

Potatoes? In a doughnut? At Tasty n Sons the answer is a resounding yes. Chef and owner John Gorham has been making this signature treat since his early cooking days at Simpatica Dining Hall, perfecting the recipe over the years. He uses potatoes to lighten the dough, similar to how spuds add pillowy levity to gnocchi or a King's Hawaiian roll. The accompanying crème anglaise is a vanilla lover's dream come true; save the extra for drizzling on cake or fresh fruit.

1 ***Make the crème anglaise:*** Create an ice-water bath in a large bowl, then set a smaller bowl fitted with a fine strainer inside. In the bowl of a stand mixer fitted with the whisk attachment, whip the egg yolks and ¼ cup of the sugar on high speed until they turn light yellow and ribbons form, 2 to 3 minutes. In a medium saucepan combine the milk, cream, remaining ¼ cup sugar, and vanilla. Cook over medium heat, stirring occasionally, until very hot but not boiling, 5 to 6 minutes. Temper the egg yolks by whisking in about half of the hot milk mixture, then pour the tempered yolks into the saucepan and cook, stirring constantly, until thickened and the mixture thickly coats the back of a spoon, 3 to 4 minutes. Remove from the heat and press through the strainer; cool in the ice-water bath, stirring occasionally. Press plastic wrap on the surface of the mixture and refrigerate until ready to use.

2 ***Make the doughnuts:*** In a medium saucepan, melt 1 tablespoon of the butter with the scraped vanilla bean seeds, then add the potatoes, ¼ cup of the sugar, and milk. Bring to a simmer and cook until the potatoes are soft, 20 minutes. Meanwhile, in a small microwave-safe bowl, combine the bittersweet and semisweet chocolate chips,

For the Crème Anglaise

5 large **egg yolks**

½ cup **sugar**

1 cup **milk**

1 cup **heavy cream**

½ **vanilla bean**, split and scraped (reserve the other half for the doughnuts)

For the Doughnuts

1½ tablespoons **unsalted butter**

½ **vanilla bean**, split and scraped

1 pound **russet potatoes**, peeled and diced (2½ cups)

¼ cup plus 6 tablespoons **sugar**

2 cups **milk**

½ cup **bittersweet chocolate chips**

½ cup **semisweet chocolate chips**

1½ teaspoons **cocoa powder**

1 large **egg**

½ cup **sour cream**

2 tablespoons **buttermilk**

Oil, for deep frying

1 cup **all-purpose flour**

1 cup **pastry flour**

1 tablespoon **baking powder**

¾ teaspoon **baking soda**

½ cup **sugar**

1 tablespoon **cinnamon**

recipe continues

cocoa powder, and the remaining ½ tablespoon of butter. Microwave on high, stirring every 45 seconds, until melted, 2 to 3 minutes. Set aside. When the potatoes are cooked, strain and discard the liquid and cool the potatoes on a baking sheet until the rest of liquid is evaporated, 10 minutes. Set aside.

3 In the bowl of a stand mixer fitted with the paddle attachment, beat the egg and the remaining 6 tablespoons sugar on medium speed until it turns pale yellow and ribbons form, 2 to 3 minutes. Add the melted chocolate, sour cream, buttermilk, and egg mixture and stir with a wooden spoon or silicone spatula until it resembles a glossy pudding.

4 When the potatoes have cooled, pass them through a food mill (or a conical strainer with a ladle) into the batter and fold until incorporated. In a separate bowl, whisk the flours, baking powder, and baking soda, then fold the flour mixture into the batter. Stir as much as possible, then use your hands to thoroughly mix the dough until it is shiny and aerated. Divide the dough into ¼-cup portions and roll into balls about 2 inches in diameter.

5 Fill a large pot halfway with oil and heat to 350°F. Combine the remaining ½ cup sugar and cinnamon in a large bowl. Set a rack over a baking sheet. Working in batches, fry the dough in the oil, turning midway through cooking, until cooked through, 5 to 6 minutes. Using a slotted spoon, transfer the doughnuts to the rack, cool for 30 seconds, then toss in the cinnamon-sugar mixture. Divide the crème anglaise among serving bowls and serve the doughnuts on top of the crème anglaise.

Mashed potatoes in doughnuts? Yes, indeed.

NEWMAN'S - ALOHA JUICE - LEMMA
Fleur de lis Bakery - CREATIVE GROWERS
OBM - VINUM - NICKY USA - OWCD
Casa Bruno - WILDSIDE - D'VINE
GALAXY - Mary's Chickens - CHOP
Zancanella - PATRICK'S BERRIES
CHEESE BAR - Carlton farms - C & G
Viola - ESTELLE - SUNSHINE DAIRY
Your Kitchen Garden - Petite Monde
UPTOWN LIQUOR - BOW and ARROW

GROUNDWORKS Organics - VIN de GARDE
VIRIDIAN FARMS - WATER AVENUE COFFEE
Columbia Empire Meats - Cameron
Breakside Brewery - Alexis Foods
Toro
Bravo - Charcuterie - SP PROVISIONS - Provvista
Real Good Food - Columbia BLANK - PDX Wi...
Pacific Coast Fruit - VERTICAL - Ma...
Ocean Beauty - J. Christopher

Special Thanks : Tasty N Sons Crew,
Pizza Friday, Little Green Pickle,
Trillium Wood, School House Electric,
Design within Reach, Schmeer Metal, Small Axe LLC, Jeff Made,
Brett Smith, Tina Lundholm, Ackerman Plumbing, Kevin Morris,
...ose's Restaurant Supply Viking Electric, Universal Fire,
Andrew Forbes Sidework PDX, Adams Refrigeration

CARAMELIZED GRAPEFRUIT
WITH BASIL SUGAR .... *Serves 2*

We fell in love with all of the breakfast food at Vitaly Paley's downtown spot, but we were especially beguiled by the simplicity of this charred grapefruit. At the restaurant it gets a quick face-down grill, but you can just as easily pass it under the broiler at home. The secret is to achieve a charred surface in as little time as possible without overcooking the interior of the grapefruit, so set your broiler as high as it will go. The game changer here is the basil sugar you whip up in an instant. Not only are basil and grapefruit a felicitous flavor combination, but also the color contrast of bright green against ruby red is about as happy as they come. Paley's chef de cuisine, recent *Top Chef* finalist "Dougie" Adams, recommends a generous helping of basil sugar: its sweetness offsets the burned and slightly bitter elements of the grilled fruit.

2 tablespoons **extra-virgin olive oil,** plus more for drizzling

1 large **ruby red grapefruit,** halved and seeded

3 large bright green, unblemished **basil leaves** (patted dry of all moisture if rinsed), plus more as needed

½ cup **sugar,** plus more as needed

Julienned **mint,** for garnish

1 Preheat the broiler on high, or a grill pan over high heat. Place the oil in a medium shallow bowl and dip the cut side of the grapefruit halves in the oil to coat well. Broil the halves (face up) or grill them (face down) until slightly charred, 5 to 6 minutes. Chill the grapefruit until very cold, at least 1 hour.

2 Meanwhile, in an electric spice grinder or coffee grinder, combine the basil and sugar. Process until the sugar is bright green, adding more sugar if the mixture clumps or is wet, or an additional basil leaf or two to achieve the desired color and flavor. Using a grapefruit knife or sharp paring knife, separate the grapefruit segments from the membranes. Drizzle olive oil on top of the grapefruit, then generously sprinkle each half with at least 2 tablespoons basil sugar. Garnish with mint.

COOK'S NOTE

Versatile and pretty, basil sugar can be stored in an airtight container for up to 1 month. Dip strawberries into it, shake up a gin or vodka cocktail that calls for an herbal element, or, better yet, dip the rim of the glass in it. For a fun twist, toss doughnuts or churros in basil sugar instead of regular cinnamon sugar.

KIMCHI PANCAKES

Serves 4

A pancake isn't always just a pancake; in the hands of the right chef, it can be something truly surprising and different. Exhibit A: a crispy, golden, savory number courtesy of chef Jenn Louis. On first glance it appears innocuous enough, but one bite tells you you've moved into another realm. "We all crave crispy and crunchy," says Louis, who adds a bit of cornmeal and cornstarch for textural intrigue. The result is a snappy brunch pancake that pays homage to Louis's love of Korean food. She recommends dipping the pancake in the reserved kimchi liquid, a daring departure from standard maple syrup.

2/3 cup **all-purpose flour**

3 tablespoons medium-grind **cornmeal,** such as Bob's Red Mill

3 tablespoons **semolina flour**

2 tablespoons **cornstarch**

1½ cups **kimchi,** drained and chopped, ¼ cup liquid reserved

1⅓ cups **ice-cold sparkling water**

½ cup plus 8 teaspoons **grapeseed** or **canola oil**

4 large **eggs**

Togarashi (Japanese chile flake blend) to taste

Lemon wedges, for serving

1   In a medium bowl, whisk together the flour, cornmeal, semolina, and cornstarch. Add the kimchi, sparkling water, and 2 tablespoons of the reserved kimchi liquid and stir to form a thick batter.

2   Heat a 6-inch nonstick skillet or crepe pan over high heat. Pour in 2 tablespoons of the oil, then ¾ cup of the batter, tilting the pan to spread the batter to the edges of the skillet. Cook until the underside is crispy and golden, 1 to 2 minutes. Flip and cook until the other side is browned, 1 to 2 more minutes. Transfer to a paper towel–lined rack to drain, then cook the remaining pancakes one at a time, using the remaining 6 tablespoons oil. Divide the pancakes among 4 plates.

3   Using 2 teaspoons of oil for each egg, cook the eggs in the skillet one at a time, sunny-side up (see page 233). Top each pancake with a fried egg, togarashi, a sprinkle of the remaining kimchi liquid, and a lemon wedge.

Chef Jenn Louis

KOKO MOCO .... *Serves 4*

At her island-cool Honolulu restaurant, chef Lee Anne Wong is celebrating the cuisine of her adopted state with dishes that honor Hawaiian traditions—but with a twist. According to Wong, the first loco moco originated on the Big Island of Hawaii in 1949, gaining favor with locals as a rib-sticking, inexpensive staple. In Wong's signature "Koko Moco," a highly seasoned, grass-fed beef patty rests on a crunchy-crusted skillet of rice; her house-made, umami-rific mushroom gravy is a vegetarian wonder.

For the Beef Patties

1 tablespoon **soy sauce**
1 tablespoon **Worcestershire sauce**
½ teaspoon **ground black pepper,** plus more for grilling
½ teaspoon **salt**
1½ pounds grass-fed **ground beef**

For the Garlic Oil

1 cup **vegetable oil**
12 large **garlic cloves,** peeled and smashed

4 cups cooked **white sticky rice**
2 teaspoons finely minced **garlic**
4 large **eggs**
2⅔ cups **Mushroom Gravy** (recipe follows)
1 **scallion,** green and white parts, minced
Togarashi
Toasted **white or black sesame seeds**

recipe continues

1 Make the beef patties: In a small bowl, whisk together the soy sauce, Worcestershire, salt and black pepper. Using your hands, massage the mixture into the ground beef until well mixed, being careful to not overwork the meat. Form the beef into four 6-ounce patties, about 4 inches in diameter and ½ inch thick. Refrigerate, covered, until needed.

2 Make the garlic oil: In a small saucepan, simmer the oil and smashed garlic cloves over low heat until the garlic begins to turn golden and the oil is fragrant, 20 to 30 minutes; cool to room temperature and remove the garlic cloves (save the cloves for another purpose if desired).

3 Make and assemble the dish: Heat 4 individual 6-inch skillets on high heat until they begin to lightly smoke (or you can use a large nonstick pan and cut the rice in quarters once finished). Add a tablespoon of garlic oil to each of the skillets (or ¼ cup oil to a large skillet, if using) and press one cup of rice into the bottom of each skillet (or all 4 cups if using a large skillet). Reduce the heat to medium-high and cook until lightly golden, 5 to 6 minutes. Add ¼ teaspoon of the minced garlic on the top of the rice and gently stir in; season with salt.

4 Meanwhile, preheat a grill or grill pan over medium heat. Season the beef patties with salt and pepper and grill the beef patties until medium rare, 3 to 4 minutes per side. While the patties are grilling, in a medium nonstick skillet, heat 1 tablespoon garlic oil over medium-high heat. Fry the eggs two at a time, sunny-side up (see page 233), and season with salt and pepper.

5 Place a cooked patty on top of each skillet, and ladle ⅔ cup gravy on top of each burger. Top with a fried egg and garnish with the sliced scallion, togarashi, salt, and toasted sesame seeds. Serve immediately.

COOK'S NOTE

Wong's recipe calls for several ingredients common in Asian kitchens, and increasingly easy to find. Maggi Seasoning is a dark, salty, deeply flavorful liquid proudly bolstered with MSG and prized for its massive *umami* punch. If you can't find it, use liquid Kitchen Bouquet instead. *Togarashi* is a catchall Japanese term for all kinds of dried hot peppers. It comes pure, or in a blend with other ingredients often referred to as *nanami* or *schichimi togarashi*.

MUSHROOM GRAVY .... *Makes 4½ cups*

1 Remove the rehydrated shiitake mushrooms from the water, squeeze out the excess liquid, and reserve the mushroom water. Slice the rehydrated shiitakes into ¼-inch thick slices and set aside.

2 In a medium saucepan, melt the butter over medium-high heat and cook the onions, stirring, until they begin to soften, 5 minutes. Add the garlic and cook for 1 minute more. Sprinkle the flour over the mixture and stir well until incorporated (it will become thick like a dough). Slowly add in the mushroom soaking liquid, stirring out any lumps with a whisk until all of the liquid has been added. Continue to whisk and cook over medium heat for 3 minutes. Stir in the Maggi Seasoning, mushroom soy sauce, sugar, and black pepper.

3 In a small saucepan, bring the cremini stems, sage, and cream to a simmer and cook until the stems are tender, 5 minutes. Puree the cream and mushroom mixture in a blender until smooth, making sure to allow steam to escape through the lid. Add the puree to the mushroom gravy pot. Bring the mushroom gravy to a boil, whisking until smooth. Transfer the gravy to the blender and puree, being careful to fill the blender pitcher only halfway and allowing steam to escape through the lid. Return the finished gravy to a clean pot.

4 In a large skillet, heat the garlic oil over high heat and add the quartered mushrooms; season with salt and pepper. Cook the mushrooms for 2 to 3 minutes, stirring often. Add the sliced shiitakes to the pan and cook until all of the mushrooms are cooked and tender and have released their water, 3 to 4 minutes more. Add the cooked mushrooms to the mushroom gravy. Keep warm or refrigerate until needed (extra gravy will keep refrigerated, for 3 to 4 days).

1 cup **dried shiitake mushroom caps,** soaked overnight in 4 cups of water

6 tablespoons **butter**

1 cup finely minced **yellow onion**

1 tablespoon minced **garlic**

⅔ cup **all-purpose flour**

3 tablespoons **Maggi Seasoning** (see Cook's Note, opposite)

3 tablespoons **mushroom soy sauce**

½ tablespoon **sugar**

1 teaspoon **freshly ground black pepper,** plus more for seasoning

3 cups **cremini mushrooms,** stemmed and quartered, stems reserved

1 tablespoon **dried sage,** or 3 tablespoons **fresh sage,** minced

1 cup **heavy cream**

3 tablespoons **garlic oil** for sautéing

Kosher salt

1 SWAN OYSTER DEPOT, SAN FRANCISCO, CA

Oysters . . . for breakfast? In San Francisco, the answer is a resounding yes. Long before this hundred-year-old institution opens its doors at 10:30 a.m., a line forms for one of the eight seats at the tiny, white-marble bar for a plate of some of the freshest bivalves in town. There may be fancier places, but none with as potent a combination of quality and character.

2 3 THE COUNTRY CAT, PORTLAND, OR

Adam and Jackie Sappington are the husband-and-wife chef owners of The Country Cat in Portland; smoked steelhead salmon eggs Benedict.

4 TADICH GRILL, SAN FRANCISCO, CA

Hangtown fry, an oyster omelet originally served to miners during the nineteenth-century San Francisco gold rush, has been on the menu at Tadich Grill for more than 160 years.

5 SEARS FINE FOOD, SAN FRANCISCO, CA

The silver-dollar pancakes at Sears Fine Food just off Union Square in San Francisco. Every order comes with precisely eighteen of the Swedish-style pancakes.

6 GRIDDLE CAFE, LOS ANGELES, CA

The Griddle Cafe, LA's hangover breakfast spot of choice. Owner Jo Kimberly's egg ring reveals her devotion to breakfast and dishes like her Tequila Sunrise (pictured).

7 BLUE STAR DONUTS, PORTLAND, OR

The Cointreau crème brulée doughnut, with a syringe of orange-scented syrup you plunge into the doughnut yourself. Call it the new injectibles.

8 FOUNTAIN COFFEE ROOM, LOS ANGELES, CA

The Fountain Coffee Room at the Beverly Hills Hotel has been an LA institution since 1949. The Fountain's nineteen barstools accommodate hip-hop moguls, Oscar winners, and regular joes for breakfast every day at the iconic curved countertop.

CHAPTER TWO

THE

MIDWEST

=== OMAHA, NE ===

OVER EASY
CHEESY BISCUITS AND VEGETARIAN
GRAVY 66

PETROW'S
CHICKEN-FRIED STEAK 69

=== KANSAS CITY, MO ===

BLUESTEM
FRUIT CREPES WITH WHIPPED CRÈME
FRAÎCHE 73

=== ST. LOUIS, MO ===

PRASINO
PRETZEL CROISSANT FRENCH TOAST
WITH TWO SAUCES 76

HALF & HALF
BAKED OATMEAL WITH RASPBERRY
COMPOTE AND CANDIED PECANS......... 79

=== CLEVELAND, OH ===

FLYING FIG
CORN AND ANDOUILLE SKILLET FRITTERS
.... 82

LUCKY'S CAFE
LEMON-BLUEBERRY WAFFLES............... 85

JACK FLAPS
GRAHAM CRACKER WAFFLES............... 88

=== CHICAGO, IL ===

ANNE SATHER
BACON CHEDDAR POTATO
PANCAKES 91

LITTLE GOAT DINER
BREAKFAST SPAGHETTI WITH CLAMS AND
CRAB 93

UNCLE MIKE'S PLACE
FILIPINO STEAK WITH GARLIC FRIED RICE
.... 94

MINDY'S HOT CHOCOLATE
BLUEBERRY AND CHEESE DANISH WITH
BROWN BUTTER STREUSEL.................. 98

PERENNIAL VIRANT
MARKET VEGETABLE OMELET WITH GOAT
CHEESE AND PESTO 102

GREAT PLAINS, GREAT PLATES

There's nothing like a long drive amid the cornfields for taking stock (not to mention giving your appetite a rest). Where else could you drive up to the window of a funky organic breakfast joint and order take-out vegetarian biscuits and gravy a few minutes' drive away from a fourth-generation steakhouse where a chicken-fried steak and strawberry shake are a standard morning order? (For the record, that place is Omaha.) We took a shine to cities like St. Louis, where we arrived expecting to eat well and left overwhelmed by the great variety of excellent food—including one of the best French toasts we'd ever had, hidden away in a shopping-mall restaurant, and a fruit-topped baked oatmeal that forever redefined "hot cereal" for us.

In Chicago, we marveled at the sheer variety of delectable options, like Stephanie Izard's surprising breakfast-spaghetti dish at the Little Goat and some of the best Filipino breakfasts we'd ever tried, courtesy of a Polish-American entrepreneur who you might say married into the business. In Cleveland, we detected prodigious talent on the sweeter side of things, which proved true in two of the best waffle creations. Another of the Midwest's common denominator? Desserts-for-breakfast that didn't skimp on creativity, but still delivered a hearty comfort-food fix.

CHEESY BISCUITS

AND VEGETARIAN GRAVY..............................*Serves 6 to 8*

We knew we were onto something special the minute we rolled up to Over Easy, hidden deep in the suburbs of West Omaha. Bright, cheery, and proud of its relationships with local purveyors, the restaurant is housed in a former Blimpie—complete with drive-thru window. Instead of doing away with a feature typically associated with a fast-food joint, owner Nick Bartholomew kept it in operation, allowing locals to order a healthy, farm-fresh breakfast on the go. We loved the biscuits and vegetarian gravy, which swap bacon grease for savory mushrooms. Trust us, you'll never miss the meat.

For the Biscuits

2¼ cups **all-purpose flour,** plus more for dusting
    the work surface

4 teaspoons **baking powder**

¼ teaspoon **baking soda**

1 teaspoon **salt**

1 teaspoon **freshly ground black pepper**

1 cup **milk**

5 tablespoons **unsalted butter,** cut into small cubes
    and softened

1 cup shredded **Italian four-cheese blend** or cheese
    of your choice

1 **scallion,** green and white parts, thinly sliced

For the Gravy

3 tablespoons **unsalted butter,** softened

1 small **onion,** finely diced (1 cup)

1 tablespoon minced **garlic**

1 tender inner **celery stalk,** finely diced

recipe continues

1 **_Make the biscuits:_** Preheat the oven to 350°F. Into a large mixing bowl, sift the flour, baking powder, baking soda, salt, and pepper. Gently stir in the milk, butter, cheese, and scallion until the dough just comes together. Turn the dough onto a floured work surface, gently shape it into a 1-inch-thick circle, and cut out 12 biscuits using a 2½-inch cookie cutter, gently gathering and rerolling excess dough. Arrange on a baking sheet and bake for 10 minutes, then rotate the pan and bake until just slightly browned, 10 to 11 more minutes. Keep warm.

2 Meanwhile, **_make the gravy:_** In a 4-quart saucepan, heat the butter over medium heat. Add the onion, garlic, celery, and carrots and cook, stirring, until caramelized, 15 minutes. Add the mushrooms and flour and cook, stirring, until the flour is absorbed into the vegetables, 2 minutes. Add the milk in a steady stream, half a cup at a time, stirring constantly and allowing the mixture to warm each time before adding more milk. Add the salt, pepper, paprika, and sour cream, stir to incorporate, then whisk in the cornstarch slurry. Cook until thickened, 2 to 3 minutes, then remove from heat.

3 In a medium skillet, cook the eggs, sunny-side up (see page 233). To serve, top 2 biscuits with a generous portion of gravy and an egg.

1 large or 2 small **carrots,** peeled and shredded
8 ounces **button mushrooms,** trimmed and thinly sliced
½ cup **all-purpose flour**
4 cups **milk**
2 teaspoons **salt**
¾ teaspoon **finely ground white pepper**
1 teaspoon **paprika**
¼ cup **sour cream**
2 tablespoons **cornstarch,** dissolved in 2 tablespoons cold water

6 large **eggs,** for serving
butter and oil, for frying

CHICKEN-FRIED STEAK .... *Serves 4*

At Petrow's, a sixty-year-old institution and gathering place for generations in this steady Midwestern town, everything seems larger than life. As East Coasters, we marveled at the sheer size of everything, from the tall steel cups used to make their classic milkshakes to the dining room, which seemed to stretch back half a city block. Omaha is a beef town, and we were here for the chicken-fried steak, made from certified Angus—custom-cut to size, tenderized, and simply seasoned before getting a coating of eggs and bread crumbs. It's true, chicken-fried steak is often a wet-battered affair, but we were beguiled by how easy—and crispy—this breaded version was. The strawberry milkshake—topped with whipped cream along with their American fries sealed the deal.

1 Season the steaks with half the smoked salt and pepper. Place the flour in a wide, shallow bowl with the remaining salt and pepper. Place the eggs in a wide, shallow bowl. Place the bread crumbs in a third shallow bowl. One at a time, dredge the steaks in the flour, shaking off the excess. Dip each steak in the eggs, then dredge both sides of each steak in the bread crumbs, pressing so the crumbs adhere.

2 Heat a large cast-iron skillet or griddle over medium-high heat. Very lightly coat the skillet with vegetable oil, and place as many steaks as will fit comfortably in the skillet. Weigh down the steaks with an additional skillet or a panini weight. Sear until browned and crisp, 5 minutes. Flip, coating the skillet with more oil and weighing down the top, and cook until the other side is crisped, an additional 5 minutes.

3 **Make the gravy:** Wipe out the skillet and heat the oil over medium heat. Add the flour, salt, and pepper and cook,

recipe continues

For the Steak:

4 7-ounce, ½-inch-thick certified Angus **top sirloin steaks,** tenderized (see Cook's Note)

1½ teaspoons **smoked salt** (or 1½ teaspoons sea salt plus 1 teaspoon smoked paprika)

2 teaspoons **freshly ground black pepper**

1 cup **all-purpose flour**

8 large **eggs,** lightly beaten

2 cups **plain dry bread crumbs**

Vegetable oil

4 large **eggs**

For the Gravy:

3 tablespoons **canola oil**

3 tablespoons **flour**

½ teaspoon **salt**

¼ teaspoon **freshly ground black pepper**

1¾ cups **whole milk,** plus more if needed

Strawberry Milkshake (recipe follows)

American Fries (recipe follows)

─────── **COOK'S NOTE** ───────

If your steaks are not pretenderized, use a meat tenderizing mallet to pound the steak on both sides until tender.

stirring with a wooden spoon, until you get a toasty, thickened, golden brown roux. Slowly add the milk and cook, whisking, until the gravy is thickened, 2–3 more minutes, adding more milk by the tablespoonful if necessary.

4 Cook the eggs, sunny-side up (see page 233), and serve with the steaks, gravy, American fries, and milkshakes.

STRAWBERRY MILKSHAKE .... *Serves 4*

Combine 1 cup of the chopped strawberries with the sugar in a small saucepan and bring to a boil while stirring. Reduce the heat and simmer until the mixture is syrupy, 5 minutes. Remove from the heat, transfer to a bowl, and chill in the refrigerator until cool to the touch, 1 hour. To make 2 milkshakes, combine half of the cooled strawberry sauce in a blender with 4 cups ice cream, 1 cup fresh chopped strawberries, and 1 cup milk. Blend until thick and creamy, 30 seconds. Divide among 2 glasses and top with whipped cream; repeat with the remaining ingredients.

3 cups chopped **strawberries,** divided

1 cup **sugar**

8 cups **vanilla ice cream**

2 cups **milk**

whipped cream, for serving

AMERICAN FRIES .... *Serves 4*

Bring a large pot of water to a boil and boil the potatoes until just tender, 25 minutes. Drain, let cool, then slice into 1/8-inch-thick rounds. Heat half the clarified butter in a large cast-iron skillet over medium-high heat. Add half the potatoes, fitting as many potatoes flat against the surface of the skillet as possible (it's okay if some do not). Season with salt, and cook until the undersides of the potatoes are brown and crispy, 3 to 4 minutes. Flip and cook until the other sides are brown and crispy, 2 to 3 minutes. Drain on paper towels, season with more salt to taste, and repeat with the remaining clarified butter and potatoes.

2 large **russet potatoes,** peeled

6 tablespoons **clarified butter** (see page 212)

Kosher salt to taste

Chicken-fried steak, and eggs, American fries, and a strawberry milkshake for breakfast at Petrow's

FRUIT CREPES

WITH WHIPPED CRÈME FRAÎCHE...................................... *Serves 8 (3 crepes per person)*

Award-winning chefs Colby and Megan Garrelts are known for food that's equally elegant and delicious, and this recipe is no exception. It's also an exercise in versatility; once you master the tender crepes, the fruit filling and sweet cream elements can be combined, as they are here, for the ultimate brunch dish. Or, if you're feeling creative, separate the elements and use them as inspiration for countless other preparations.

1 **Make the filling:** In a medium saucepan with a tight-fitting lid, combine 1½ cups water with the cider, brandy, fruit, and sugar. Cover, bring to a boil over medium-high heat, then lower the heat and cook on medium-low until the fruit is tender, 15 to 20 minutes. Using a slotted spoon, remove the poached fruit, reserving the liquid, and cool slightly. Cut the flesh off the fruit, discarding the stems and core.

2 In a blender, puree the fruit with just enough of the cooking liquid (1 to 1½ cups) to make a smooth puree, 30 seconds. Discard any remaining cooking liquid, then transfer the puree to the saucepan and bring to a boil over medium-high heat. Reduce the heat and simmer, stirring occasionally, until the puree thickens and turns translucent, 30 minutes. Stir in the lemon juice, transfer to a bowl, cool slightly, then cover and refrigerate until chilled and slightly thickened, at least 2 hours or overnight (extra filling will keep, refrigerated, for up to 1 month).

3 **Prepare the fruit and crème fraîche:** In a medium bowl, toss together the pears, sugar, cinnamon, vanilla, and

recipe continues

For the Fruit Filling

½ cup **apple cider**

½ cup **brandy**

3 **quinces, apples, or pears,** peeled

1 cup **sugar**

3 tablespoons **fresh lemon juice**

For the Fruit and Crème Fraîche

2 firm, ripe **pears,** peeled, cored, and thinly sliced

4 teaspoons **sugar**

1 teaspoon **cinnamon**

2 teaspoons **vanilla extract**

½ teaspoon **freshly grated nutmeg**

1 tablespoon **unsalted butter**

½ cup **heavy cream**

1 cup **crème fraîche** or sour cream

2 tablespoons **honey,** plus more for drizzling

24 **Crepes** (recipe follows)

fresh raspberries and **pear slices** for garnish

nutmeg. In a medium skillet, melt the butter over low heat, add the pears, and cook until tender, 8 to 9 minutes. Remove from the heat and set aside.

4 In the bowl of a stand mixer, whisk the cream until soft peaks form, 1 to 2 minutes. Gently fold in the crème fraîche and honey.

5 To assemble the crepes, arrange a crepe on a flat work surface and smear with 2 tablespoons of the fruit filling. Layer ¼ cup cooked pears over the filling, then dollop with ¼ cup of the whipped crème fraîche. Fold the crepe in quarters and repeat with the remaining crepes. Arrange the crepes on dessert plates and drizzle with honey. Garnish with raspberries, pear slices, and additional whipped cream.

CREPES .... *Makes 24 crepes*

1 In a blender, blend the flour, eggs, 1½ cups water, milk, and salt on high speed until smooth, 15 to 30 seconds. Transfer the batter to an airtight container and chill for at least 2 hours or overnight.

2 Coat a nonstick 8-inch crepe pan or skillet with cooking spray or butter and heat over medium heat. Ladle in 2 to 3 tablespoons batter, swirl to coat the pan, and cook until the crepe begins to bubble slightly, pulls away from the sides, and turns golden underneath, 1 minute per side. Transfer the crepe to a plate and repeat with the remaining batter, layering paper towels between crepes. Cover with plastic wrap until ready to use. (Crepes can be frozen between layers of waxed paper, sealed tightly in plastic wrap, for up to 3 months.)

2 cups **all-purpose flour**
2 large **eggs**
1 cup **whole milk**
1 teaspoon **kosher salt**
Cooking spray or butter

Al's Breakfast, Minneapolis

"This is only the third grill they've installed since opening in 1950," said Alison Kirwin from across the yellow Formica countertop as she flipped pancakes on the giant, sizzling flattop at Al's Breakfast in the Dinkytown neighborhood of Minneapolis. Ask locals where to go for morning eats, and pretty much everyone directs you here. There's something about Al's fourteen humble barstools—not to mention a no-favorites, first-come, first-served waiting policy—that democratizes the experience here, attracting a cross-section of city residents, ranging from hungover U of M students who end a night on the town by waiting for the doors to open at 6:00 a.m. to machinists ready to power up before a day of heavy labor. Original owner Al Bergstrom allowed railroad workers to prepay for vouchers when they were flush with cash; the tradition continues today, and anyone can plunk down some cash and create a tab at Al's.

The short-order food hasn't changed much in the past sixty-six years—blueberry pancakes and bacon waffles endure—but there's a meticulousness to the preparation and presentation of food you might not expect. "People want things to be the way they had them last time," said Kirwin as she beat half-and-half into eggs destined for an omelet. She jokingly refers to line-cook duties as "bottom of the barrel" but still fulfills the role regularly, even though she's now a manager. As locals pored over the local paper—sometimes being moved to another seat midmeal to keep the line moving—we could feel a rhythm built into a morning at Al's; the clink of silverware and the steam hissing off that grill are as much a soundtrack as the jazz wafting from Kirwin's radio. It stays busy nonstop until Al's closes at 1 p.m., but Minneapolis can be sure the popular restaurant will see another day.

CENTER: Meal tickets

BOTTOM: Manager and cook Alison Kirwin

PRETZEL CROISSANT FRENCH TOAST

WITH TWO SAUCES..*Serves 6*

We'd tried a lot of French toast by the time we arrived at Prasino, but this one sounded so special, we had to try it, too. While some recipes bog down the bread, Prasino's version gives the salty pretzel croissants a very brief dip before cooking, yielding an airy end result. Just before serving, they're topped with a duo of home-made, surprisingly simple sauces. If you can't find pretzel croissants, high-quality traditional ones will do just fine.

1 **Make the caramel:** In a heavy-bottomed saucepan over medium-low heat, cook the sugar and cream of tartar, watching carefully and swirling the pot occasionally (do not stir) until the sugar caramelizes and turns amber, 6 to 7 minutes. Carefully whisk in the cream (it will bubble), then add the butter a few cubes at a time. Add the salt, remove from the heat, and let cool to room temperature.

2 **Make the white chocolate sauce:** Place the white chocolate chips in a heat-proof bowl. In a small saucepan, heat the cream until it begins to simmer. Pour the cream over the chocolate, wait 1 minute, then stir until smooth.

3 **Make the French toast:** In a large, shallow bowl, whisk together the eggs, half-and-half, sugar, salt, and vanilla. In a large skillet, gently heat 2 tablespoons of the butter over medium-low heat. Dip the croissants briefly in the batter, shaking off excess. Working in batches, fry the croissants, adding more butter if needed, until browned and crisped, 3 minutes per side. Arrange 2 French toast halves on each plate and drizzle generously with the caramel and white chocolate sauces.

For the Caramel Sauce

2¼ cups **sugar**
Pinch of **cream of tartar**
¾ cup **heavy cream**
5 tablespoons cold **unsalted butter,** cubed
1 teaspoon **sea salt**

For the White Chocolate Sauce

1½ cups **white chocolate chips**
¾ cup **heavy cream**

For the French Toast

4 large **eggs**
¼ cup **half-and-half**
1 teaspoon **sugar**
¾ teaspoon **sea salt**
1½ tablespoons **vanilla extract**
4 tablespoons (½ stick) **unsalted butter** or canola oil, plus more as needed, for frying
6 store-bought **pretzel croissants,** halved

—— **COOK'S NOTE** ——
Sauces will keep, refrigerated in airtight containers, for up to 2 weeks. Warm extra sauce and use as a topping over ice cream, cake, or fruit.

St. Louis Specialties

Every town has its morning-hour food favorites, and St. Louis has two of the most distinctive. We first came across the Slinger at Eat-Rite, a former chain of counter-style diners that only has one remaining location in town. The white cinderblock cube, complete with pinball machine and Formica countertop, sits on the path of the original, iconic Route 66.

Though we were there early in the morning, we quickly learned that we'd missed prime Slinger hours: 1:00 to 4:00 a.m., when bars let out and patrons seek this hangover cure. "It always seems like a good idea at the time of ordering," said Joe Holleman, a lifetime St. Louis resident and a columnist for the *St. Louis Post-Dispatch*, who cops to having eaten his fair share of post-revelry Slingers. That's no surprise, considering its contents: "It always includes over-easy eggs, chopped hamburger bits, chili, hash brown potatoes, raw chopped onions—and sometimes shredded cheese," said Holleman, who sounded full just describing the dish.

There's also a debate about who first invented another St. Louis original, the gooey butter cake. Tradition has it that an unwitting baker swapped the proportions of flour and butter in a coffee cake, yielding sticky, chewy bars that some may have deemed inedible. Being frugal Midwesterners, they opted to sell their mistakes instead of discarding them—and a new dessert classic was born. Though there are many recipes for locals they're a strictly purchase-only treat. We loved the name of a competing spot, Gooey Louie, but tried ours at the Park Avenue Coffee House downtown. There, the moist, sweet square, which came in flavors ranging from amaretto to white chocolate, made gooey lovers out of all of us.

TOP: A waitress at Eat-Rite with a slinger, the ultimate hangover food

BOTTOM: A gooey butter cake at Park Avenue Coffee House

BAKED OATMEAL
WITH RASPBERRY COMPOTE AND CANDIED PECANS ....*Serves 4*

We never looked at a bowl of oatmeal the same way again after sampling the fruity, chewy, and entirely satisfying version made at Half & Half, a cozy-chic spot in suburban Clayton. Truly a meal in a mug, it starts with good old-fashioned rolled oats cooked slow and low to perfection. Berry compote, candied nuts, fresh fruit, and maple syrup top off the grains. We recommend you add grapes to the mix; heating them for a few minutes brings out their juicy sweetness.

¼ cup **pecans**

½ cup **sugar**

¾ teaspoon **salt,** plus more for seasoning

2 tablespoons **unsalted butter**

2½ cups **old-fashioned rolled oats,** such as Bob's Red Mill

2½ cups **whole milk**

1½ cups **raspberries,** fresh or frozen and thawed

1 cup **fresh fruit** (such as grapes, blueberries, blackberries, quartered strawberries)

Maple syrup, for serving

1   In a small skillet over medium-low heat, combine the pecans, ⅓ cup of the sugar, and a pinch of salt and cook, stirring, until the sugar melts into a caramel, 3 minutes. Add the butter carefully and swirl the skillet to coat the pecans well. Cool slightly, then transfer the pecans to a cutting board and roughly chop. Set aside.

2   In a medium saucepan, bring the oats, milk, 2½ cups water, and ¾ teaspoon salt to a simmer and cook, stirring often, until the oats are tender and have absorbed all of the liquid, 20 minutes.

3   While the oats are cooking, in a small saucepan, gently simmer the raspberries with the rest of the sugar and a pinch of salt until the raspberries release their juices and thicken slightly without losing their shape, 3 to 4 minutes. Cover to keep warm.

recipe continues

4 Preheat the oven to 450°F. Divide the warm cooked oatmeal among 4 ovenproof coffee mugs or bowls. Top with raspberry compote and fresh fruit. Arrange the mugs on a baking sheet and bake until bubbly, 9 to 10 minutes. Remove from the oven, top with the pecans and drizzle with maple syrup, then submerge the pecans in the oatmeal using a knife or chopstick. Serve each mug on a saucer to avoid burning your hands.

TOP: A server with Half & Half's famous pancakes

BOTTOM: Owner Elizabeth Randolph

CORN AND ANDOUILLE SKILLET FRITTERS ....*Serves 8*

Since 1999, chef and owner Karen Small has been serving seasonal, sustainable food in Ohio City, a historic neighborhood that's become a hub for some of Cleveland's best restaurants. These skillet-cooked fritters are made rich, smoky, and spicy with the addition of smoked paprika and andouille sausage. Fresh corn kernels add a juicy pop of sweetness, while the sausage releases its spicy oil when cooked, turning the fritters a lovely shade of orangey red. Add a poached egg, an easy hollandaise, and maple syrup, and you've achieved brunch nirvana.

1 ***Make the hollandaise:*** Fill a pot with 2 inches of water and bring to a boil, then keep the water at a low simmer. In a heatproof bowl, vigorously whisk the egg yolks, lemon juice, and maple syrup until thick and fluffy, 2 minutes. Place the bowl above the simmering water, making sure the bowl does not touch the water, and continue whipping until the sauce is warm to the touch, being careful not to overcook the eggs. Add the butter in a slow drizzle, constantly whisking, until a creamy, emulsified sauce is formed, then stir in the chile. Remove pan from heat and keep bowl warm over the hot water.

2 ***Make the fritters:*** In a medium bowl, whisk the flour, sugar, baking powder, salt, and paprika. In another bowl, whisk the milk, eggs, butter, and cheese. Add the dry ingredients to the wet and mix until just combined, making sure not to overmix. Fold in the sausage, corn, and thyme.

recipe continues

For the Hollandaise

8 large **egg yolks**

1 tablespoon **fresh lemon juice**

2 tablespoons **maple syrup**

2 sticks (½ pound) **unsalted butter,** melted

½ **red Fresno chile,** minced

For the Fritters

2 cups **all-purpose flour**

¼ cup **sugar**

1½ tablespoons **baking powder**

1 teaspoon **salt**

1 teaspoon **hot smoked paprika**

1 cup **whole milk**

2 large **eggs**

8 tablespoons (1 stick) **unsalted butter,** melted, plus more for brushing the skillet

1 cup grated **Cheddar cheese**

1 **andouille** or other smoked, spicy sausage link, diced (½ cup)

½ cup **fresh corn kernels** (from 1 cob), or ½ cup frozen kernels, thawed

1 tablespoon **fresh thyme leaves,** chopped

8 large **eggs**

Maple syrup, for serving

Chopped **chives** for garnish

3 Heat a griddle or a cast-iron skillet over medium-low heat and brush with butter. Working in batches, spoon ¼ cup batter for each fritter into the skillet, spreading the batter into round or oval shapes. Cook the fritters until bubbles form, 3 to 4 minutes, then flip and cook until the underside is browned, an additional 3 to 4 minutes. Repeat with the remaining batter. Prepare a medium pot of water for poached eggs. Poach and drain the eggs (see page 231).

4 To serve, arrange 2 fritters on a plate and top with a poached egg, hollandaise to taste, and a drizzle of maple syrup. Garnish with chives.

Flying Fig chef/owner Karen Small

LEMON-BLUEBERRY WAFFLES .... *Serves 8*

We were turned on to Lucky's Cafe by none other than our friend, superstar chef Michael Symon, who raved about the expertly made breakfasts—and decidedly Midwestern portions. We arrived there on game day—Cleveland's beloved Browns were taking on the Ravens in a few hours—and the place quickly filled up with jersey-clad patrons whose allegiance to Lucky's seemed to match (or exceed) their ardor for the local team. For us, the clear winner was the light, airy lemon waffles topped with blueberries, sweetened cream, and a decadent lemon curd. While most curds are thickened on the stovetop, we loved chef-owner Heather Haviland's method for baking the curd in the oven, freeing up your hands to get going with other elements of the dish.

For the Lemon Curd

1 14-ounce can **sweetened condensed milk**
½ cup **sour cream**
6 large **egg yolks**
¼ teaspoon **kosher salt**
¾ cup **fresh lemon juice**

For the Blueberry Compote

¾ cup **sugar**
3 cups **fresh blueberries**
Juice and grated zest of 1 **lemon**

1 **Make the lemon curd:** Preheat the oven to 325°F. In the bowl of a stand mixer fitted with the whisk attachment, beat the sweetened condensed milk, sour cream, egg yolks, and salt on medium-high speed until incorporated, 1 minute. Reduce the speed to low, add the lemon juice, and beat until gradually incorporated. Pour the mixture into a 10-inch pie pan and bake until slightly thickened, 12 minutes. Place on a rack and cool completely. Press through a sieve into a bowl, cover with plastic wrap, and refrigerate until chilled, 2 hours.

2 **Make the compote:** In a small (1-quart) heavy-bottomed saucepan, bring the sugar and ⅓ cup water to a boil, reduce the heat, and simmer until slightly thickened, 1 minute. Stir in the blueberries and simmer, stirring occasionally, until the berries begin to burst, 3 to 4 minutes. Remove from the heat and stir in the lemon juice and zest.

recipe continues

3 ***Make the honeyed whipped cream:*** Chill the bowl of an electric stand mixer for 20 minutes. Fit the bowl with the whisk attachment and beat the cream, honey, and salt on low speed for 1 minute. Increase the speed to medium and whip until ribbons form, 2 minutes. Increase the speed to medium-high and whip until stiff peaks form, 30 seconds. Transfer to a serving bowl and set aside. Cover and chill until serving.

4 ***Make the waffles:*** Sift the flour, baking powder, and salt into a medium bowl. In the bowl of a stand mixer fitted with the whisk attachment, beat the buttermilk, sugar, honey, eggs, and vanilla on low speed until blended, 1 minute. Add the butter, lemon juice, and zest and beat until combined, 1 minute. Replace the whisk with the paddle attachment, add the dry ingredients, and mix just until incorporated, 30 seconds.

5 Preheat a waffle iron and coat lightly with cooking spray. Pour 1/2 cup of the batter into the waffle iron, spreading to evenly distribute the batter. Close the lid and bake according to the manufacturer's instructions, until the waffle is lightly browned and crisp. Repeat with the remaining batter, brushing the finished waffles with the melted butter. Serve the waffles topped with the blueberry compote, honeyed whipped cream, and lemon curd. Garnish with mint.

For the Honeyed Whipped Cream

1 cup **heavy cream**
2 tablespoons **honey**
Pinch of **kosher salt**

For the Lemon Waffles

3½ cups **all-purpose flour**
4 teaspoons **baking powder**
¼ teaspoon **kosher salt**
1½ cups **buttermilk,** preferably higher-fat
1/3 cup **sugar**
1/3 cup **honey**
2 large **eggs**
2 teaspoons **vanilla extract**
8 tablespoons (1 stick) **unsalted butter,** melted and cooled
Juice and zest of 1 **lemon**
Cooking spray

4 tablespoons (½ stick) **unsalted butter,** melted, for serving
Fresh **mint leaves** and **toasted sliced almonds** for garnish

Sumptuous lemon waffles topped three ways at Lucky's in Cleveland

GRAHAM CRACKER WAFFLES

..................Serves 8

A Nutella s'more was Eric Williams's inspiration for this decadent waffle—one of several at his award-winning Cleveland breakfast and lunch joint—which puts a fresh spin on a classic flavor. The waffle base itself, which is generously laced with baking powder for rise and cornstarch for crispness, has become our new standard-bearer for the waffle category—a campfire favorite in sit-down, knife-and-fork form.

For the Nutella Sauce (makes 2 cups)

1 cup **heavy cream**

1 cup **Nutella** spread

¼ teaspoon **cinnamon**

Pinch of **kosher salt**

For the Waffle Batter

2½ cups **all-purpose flour**

2 tablespoons **cornstarch**

2 tablespoons **baking powder**

¼ teaspoon **kosher salt**

2 large **eggs,** separated

¼ cup **sugar**

1 cup **whole milk**

¾ cup **buttermilk**

1½ teaspoons **vanilla extract**

3 tablespoons **unsalted butter,** melted, plus more
    for brushing the waffle iron

2 cups crushed **graham crackers**

4 cups **mini marshmallows**

recipe continues

1 ***Make the Nutella sauce:*** In a blender, combine the cream, Nutella, cinnamon, and salt and puree until smooth; transfer to a bowl and set aside.

2 ***Make the waffle batter:*** Preheat the oven to 250°F. In a large bowl, sift the flour, cornstarch, baking powder, and salt; reserve. In the bowl of a stand mixer fitted with the whisk attachment, whip the egg whites and sugar on high speed until soft peaks form, 2 to 3 minutes; set aside.

3 Meanwhile, in a separate bowl, whisk the egg yolks, milk, buttermilk, and vanilla until blended. Add the wet ingredients to the dry and mix with a rubber spatula until well combined. Stir in the butter, then gently fold in the egg whites until just incorporated.

4 Brush the waffle iron with melted butter. Pour ½ cup of the batter into the waffle iron, using a spatula to ensure it is evenly distributed, and cook according to the manufacturer's instructions, 3 to 4 minutes. Transfer the cooked waffles to a baking sheet and keep warm in the oven; repeat with the remaining batter.

5 Remove the baking sheet from the oven while you preheat the broiler. Top each waffle with ¼ cup Nutella sauce, ¼ cup crushed graham crackers, and ½ cup mini marshmallows. Place the waffles under the broiler until the marshmallows melt and are slightly charred, 20 to 30 seconds. Serve immediately.

LEFT TO RIGHT: Jack Flaps' funky interior; owner Eric Williams

BACON CHEDDAR POTATO PANCAKES

Makes 10 pancakes

Named for its previous owner, whose beatific portrait hangs in the entrance of the location we visited in Chicago's Belmont neighborhood, this small chain was bought in 1981 by young entrepreneur Tom Tunney, who still runs the business today. We loved the Swedish folk-art murals by artist Sigmund Arseth hanging above us almost as much as these dilly, cheesy potato pancakes, which we adapted for lazy weekend mornings with the help of a surprising ingredient—boxed potato pancake mix.

1 In a large bowl, whisk the potato pancake mix, flour, baking powder, salt, and pepper. Mix in the eggs and 3 1/4 cups cold water with a wooden spoon until incorporated, then add the cheese, bacon, potato, onion, and dill.

2 Heat a griddle or cast-iron skillet over medium heat and butter generously. In batches, ladle 1/2 cup batter onto the griddle and spread to a 6-inch round.

3 Cook until bubbles form all over the pancake and the edges are lacy and golden, 4 minutes. Flip and cook until the pancake is cooked through, 4 more minutes. Repeat with the remaining butter. To serve, top the pancakes with sour cream and dill.

One 6-ounce package **potato pancake mix** (see Cook's Note)

1 1/4 cups **self-rising flour**

5 teaspoons **baking powder**

1/2 tablespoon **salt**

1 teaspoon **freshly ground black pepper**

2 **eggs**, beaten

1 1/4 cups grated **Cheddar cheese**

2/3 cup chopped cooked **bacon**

1/2 cup finely diced **potato**

1/2 cup grated **onion**

1/2 cup chopped **fresh dill**, plus more for serving

Melted butter, for cooking

Sour cream, for serving

─── **COOK'S NOTE** ───

Potato pancake mix is available in the kosher aisle of most regular supermarkets, or can be ordered on Amazon.com.

BREAKFAST SPAGHETTI
WITH CLAMS AND CRAB .... *Serves 2*

Pasta for breakfast seems altogether reasonable in the hands of chef Stephanie Izard. Here, her take on spaghetti alla vongole (spaghetti with clams) involves the surprising element of eggs, used to bind the spaghetti "cake" and over-easy, cooked right in to blend with the clams, sorrel, and crab, creating a sort of free-form seafood sauce. Try to get a good-quality clam stock from your local fishmonger, or use the liquid leftover from steaming the clams to make your own.

1 Bring a large pot of water to a boil. Salt the water and add the spaghetti, cooking according to the package directions, until al dente. Drain the pasta, transfer to a bowl, and toss with the Parmesan and beaten egg.

2 Heat 2 small nonstick skillets over medium heat, then coat each pan with ½ tablespoon of the butter. Divide the spaghetti between the skillets, covering the entire bottom of the pan. Form a nest in the center of each skillet. Cook over low heat until the spaghetti begins to brown, 6 to 7 minutes. Crack an egg into each nest and cook until the whites set, 4 minutes. Using a rubber spatula, flip and cook until the yolks are over-easy, 15 to 20 seconds. Flip back into warmed bowls.

3 Meanwhile, in a large skillet, reduce the clam stock by half over medium-high heat, 6 to 7 minutes. Whisk in the remaining 2 tablespoons butter, add the bok choy, and cook until wilted, 1 to 2 minutes. Add the lemon juice, clams, and crabmeat and cook, tossing gently, until heated through, 1 minute. Season with salt and pepper, divide among the 2 bowls of spaghetti, and garnish with the sorrel.

Kosher salt

4 ounces **dry spaghetti**

2 tablespoons grated **Parmigiano-Reggiano cheese**

1 large **egg**, beaten, plus 2 **whole eggs**

3 tablespoons **unsalted butter,** divided

½ cup good-quality **clam stock**

½ cup sliced **bok choy** (green parts only)

4 teaspoons **fresh lemon juice**

1 dozen **clams,** steamed and shucked (see Cook's Note)

2 tablespoons picked **crabmeat**

Freshly ground black pepper to taste

¼ cup **packed sorrel** or spinach leaves, cut into thin ribbons

COOK'S NOTE
To remove the meat from fresh clams, steam the clams covered in a pot of shallow boiling water until the shells open, 5 to 6 minutes. Cool slightly, then pull the clams from the shells.

TOP LEFT: The spaghetti in this dish lends a chewy texture.

BOTTOM: The bakery bar at Little Goat

FILIPINO STEAK

WITH GARLIC FRIED RICE ....*Serves 4*

How does a half-Ukrainian, half-Polish Chicago native end up cooking some of the Windy City's most celebrated Filipino food? Fall in love with a woman from Manila, that's how. In 1991 Mike Grajewski—already married to Lucia—scraped together the $25,000 down payment to buy an abandoned restaurant in the Ukrainian Village neighborhood, leaving behind his career as a scrapyard metalworker. He started out serving traditional American fare, over time adding more Filipino items as word spread about Uncle Mike's killer breakfasts. He learned by osmosis, gleaning tips from his mother-in-law and adding his own unique touches. Here, skirt steak becomes tender after an overnight bath in teriyaki and 7Up, fried rice packs a garlicky punch, and a dipping sauce originally made with fish sauce gets a vinegar swap-in and the nickname "Filipino Pico de Gallo."

1 **Prepare the steak:** Using a sharp knife, score the steak in a small cross-hatch pattern to enable better marinating. In a resealable plastic bag or nonreactive container, combine the teriyaki marinade, 7Up, and garlic. Add the steak, seal or cover tightly, and refrigerate for up to 24 hours.

2 Remove the steak from the refrigerator about an hour before you want to grill and let it come to room temperature. Heat an outdoor grill or grill pan over medium-high heat. Shake excess marinade from the steak and cook until the meat reaches 135°F for medium-rare (or higher, to your preference), 4 to 5 minutes per side.

For the Steak

2 pounds **skirt steak,** silver skin removed (ask your butcher to do this)

¾ cup **bottled teriyaki marinade**

2½ cups **7Up soda**

15 **garlic cloves,** peeled and mashed

For the Garlic Fried Rice

2 tablespoons **vegetable oil**

10 **garlic cloves,** finely chopped

3 cups **cooked jasmine rice** (1 cup raw)

1 teaspoon **kosher salt**

1 teaspoon **toasted sesame oil,** or more to taste

For the Sauce

1 medium **tomato,** finely diced

½ small **onion,** finely diced

1 tablespoon chopped **fresh cilantro**

1 tablespoon **white vinegar** (or fish sauce, if desired)

8 large **eggs**

3 ***Make the rice and the sauce:*** In a large skillet, heat the olive oil over medium-low heat. Add the garlic and fry, stirring, until fragrant, 1 to 2 minutes. Add the rice and cook, stirring, until it begins to brown and crackle, 5 minutes. Stir in the salt and sesame oil. In a small bowl, combine the tomato, onion, cilantro, and white vinegar.

4 Cook the eggs in your desired style (see page 231–233).

5 ***Plate the dish:*** Serve the steak with the rice, topped with the eggs. Serve the dipping sauce on the side.

Owners Mike and Lucia Grajewski

Other dishes at Uncle Mike's include must-orders marinated monkfish (top right) and wine-cured pork shoulder and longanisa sausage (bottom).

BLUEBERRY AND CHEESE DANISH

WITH BROWN BUTTER STREUSEL .... *Makes 6*

The name of Mindy Segal's bakery-cum-restaurant in Wicker Park is misleadingly narrow-casted. While it's true that Segal serves some of the richest, thickest hot chocolate we've tasted, she's a masterful pastry chef with a Midas touch. Everything, from Segal's house-made bagels (which give New York's best a run for their money) to her indulgent cakes and pies, is irresistible. On the summer day we arrived at her spacious dessert bar, she was in the process of taking ripe blueberries and transforming them into these flaky, cream-filled tarts. After sampling a whole host of her creations, we landed on these as our favorites. Yes, they're quite a bit of work, but trust us, they're worth it.

For the Tartlet Dough

2 sticks (½ pound) **butter**, cut into ½-inch cubes and chilled, plus more for greasing the bowl

1 **egg**

2 tablespoons **honey** (orange blossom or clover)

½ cup **whole milk**

2¼ cups **bread flour**

¾ cup **cake flour**

1½ tablespoons **sugar**

½ tablespoon **instant dry yeast**

½ teaspoon **kosher salt**

1 **Make the tartlet dough:** Grease a large bowl and set aside. In a small bowl whisk together the eggs, honey, 1 cup of cool water, and milk and set aside.

2 In a food processor, pulse the cold butter, flour, sugar, yeast, and salt until the butter is partially incorporated into the flour (about 20 pulses; there should be chunks of butter still in the mixture).

3 Add the egg mixture and pulse until a wet dough forms (about 10 pulses). Transfer the dough with a spatula to the greased bowl, and allow it to double in size, 1 hour. Wrap in plastic and refrigerate overnight.

recipe continues

BOTTOM RIGHT: The restaurant's signature beverage—hot chocolate—served with a house-made marshmallow

BOTTOM LEFT: A variety of Segal's sweet creations

4 *Make the filling:* Preheat the oven to 325°F. In the bowl of a stand mixer fitted with a paddle attachment, beat the cream cheese on medium speed until smooth, 2 minutes. Scrape the bowl down, then add the sugar and beat until fluffy, 2 minutes.

5 Stop the mixer and scrape down the bowl. Add the sour cream, egg, cream, and vanilla and beat on medium-low until smooth, 1 minute. Place the custard in an 8 x 8-inch baking pan set over a water bath and bake until the custard is set, 25 to 30 minutes. Refrigerate until cold, 1 hour or overnight.

6 *Make the streusel:* In a medium bowl, combine the flour, sugar, brown sugar, rolled oats, and salt, and set aside. Heat the butter in a small saucepan over medium heat until the milk solids begin to brown and the butter foams and gives off the aroma of toasted nuts, 7 minutes. Let the browned butter cool for 10 minutes.

7 Pour the browned butter slowly over the flour mixture, using not more than 5 tablespoons of the butter and discarding any remaining butter and solids. Rub the flour and butter between your fingers until a crumble mixture forms. Set the mixture aside and cover with plastic wrap.

8 *Macerate the berries:* In a medium saucepan, cook the blueberries with the sugar, juices, and orange blossom water, if using, until the sugar is dissolved and the liquid has boiled and thickened a bit, 6 to 8 minutes; set aside.

9 *Form and bake the tartlets:* Dust a work surface generously with flour. Turn the dough onto the work surface, dust the dough and rolling pin with flour, and roll out the dough into an approximately 16 x 11-inch rectangle.

For the Filling

1 package (8 ounces) **cream cheese,** at room temperature
¼ cup **granulated sugar**
½ cup **sour cream**
1 **egg,** at room temperature
1 tablespoon **heavy cream**
1 teaspoon **vanilla extract**

For the Streusel

¾ cup **all-purpose flour**
2½ tablespoons **sugar**
2½ tablespoons (packed) **brown sugar**
¼ cup **rolled oats**
¼ teaspoon **kosher salt**
½ cup (1 stick) **butter**

For the Macerated Blueberries

1 pint **blueberries**
¼ cup **sugar**
1 tablespoon **fresh orange juice**
1 tablespoon **fresh lemon juice**
2 drops **orange blossom water** (optional)

Flour, for dusting the work surface

10 Fold the dough into thirds like a letter (bringing the bottom third up to middle, then overlapping it with the top third). Turn the dough a half turn to the right and repeat the letter procedure. Roll and fold a total of three turns.

11 Wrap the dough in plastic wrap, and let it rest in the refrigerator for at least an hour and up to overnight. On a floured surface or on a piece of parchment paper, roll the dough approximately ¼-inch thick to a 18 x 12-inch rectangle. Place the dough on a baking sheet, cover loosely with plastic wrap, and chill approximately 1 hour in the refrigerator.

12 Preheat the oven to 375°F. Cover a baking sheet with foil and set aside. Depending on the desired size, cut the dough to fit a tart ring (six 4-inch tart pans with separate bottoms, discarding leftover dough) and form into tart shells. Let the tarts sit out at room temperature for 30 minutes.

13 Spread 2 tablespoons of the cream cheese custard evenly into each tartlet (reserve leftover custard for another use), then spoon ¼ cup of the blueberry mixture on top of that using mostly the blueberry solids. Sprinkle generously with the streusel.

14 Place the tartlets on the prepared baking sheet and bake them for 15 minutes, until the rims begin to brown. Rotate the pan, reduce the heat to 350°F, and bake for another 20 to 25 minutes, until the tartlets are golden and slightly bubbly; let cool before taking out of the pans and serving.

Chef/owner Mindy Segal

MARKET VEGETABLE OMELET

WITH GOAT CHEESE AND PESTO .... *Serves 4*

It's only fitting that Perennial Virant sits directly across from Chicago's Green City Market. The restaurant's talented chef, Paul Virant, cooks from the season's bounty, then preserves an equal amount of produce to use the rest of the year. This gorgeous dish features a summery pesto you can freeze in ice-cube trays—just pop out a cube when you're ready to cook—and easy-to-execute pickled vegetables that will keep in the fridge for a day or so.

1 ***Make the pickled vegetables:*** Spread the zucchini in an 8 × 10-inch glass dish and cover with the onion. Whisk together the lemon juice and zest, ¼ cup of the olive oil, and ¼ teaspoon each of the salt and pepper. Pour over the vegetables and marinate for 2 hours at room temperature, then refrigerate for 1 hour and up to 24 hours. Add the radishes and carrots, the remaining 1 tablespoon olive oil, and ¼ teaspoon each salt and pepper. Toss gently and set aside.

2 ***Make the omelets:*** Heat a heavy-bottomed nonstick 6- to 8-inch skillet over medium-low heat. Heat 1 tablespoon of the butter until it melts and the pan is so hot that it hisses when you add a drop of water to the skillet. Beat the eggs with salt and white pepper and add a quarter of them to the skillet, resisting the urge to stir. Cook until the bottom starts to set, 45 seconds to 1 minute. With a heat-resistant rubber spatula, gently push one edge of the egg into the center of the pan, while tilting the pan to allow the uncooked portion to flow underneath. Repeat with the other edges until there's no liquid left and the eggs resemble a bright yellow pancake.

For the Pickled Vegetables

½ pound **zucchini,** thinly sliced
    lengthwise
1 small **onion,** thinly sliced
Juice and finely grated zest
    of 2 **lemons**
¼ cup plus 1 tablespoon **olive oil**
½ teaspoon **kosher salt**
½ teaspoon **freshly ground**
    black pepper
½ pound **radishes,** thinly sliced
½ pound **carrots,** thinly sliced

For the Omelets

4 tablespoons (½ stick)
    unsalted butter
12 large **eggs**
Salt and **white pepper** to taste
½ cup **Pesto** (recipe follows)
½ cup crumbled **chèvre**
8 slices **smoked turkey breast**
    (optional)

——— COOK'S TIP ———
Use a handheld mandoline to make slicing the vegetables a breeze.

3 Gently flip the omelet, using your spatula to ease it over if necessary. Add 2 tablespoons pesto across the center of the eggs in a straight line, then crumble 2 tablespoons chèvre evenly over the entire length of the pesto. With the spatula, lift one edge of the omelet and fold it across and over, so that the edges line up, making sure not to overcook or brown the eggs. If necessary, flip the entire omelet over to finish it for 30 seconds. Gently transfer the finished omelet to a plate, garnish with 2 slices of turkey, if using, and top with 1 cup of the marinated vegetables. Repeat with the remaining ingredients to make 3 more omelets.

PESTO .... *Makes 1½ cups*

Combine all of the ingredients in a food processor and process until smooth, scraping down the sides of the bowl once or twice, 1 to 2 minutes. Store in an airtight container in the refrigerator for up to 5 days, or freeze in ice-cube trays, then pop out and store in freezer bags for up to 3 months.

8 cups lightly packed **fresh basil leaves**

¾ cup **grapeseed** or other neutral-flavored oil

1 tablespoon **pine nuts**

½ **garlic clove**

½ cup finely grated **Parmigiano-Reggiano cheese**

¼ teaspoon **kosher salt**

MORE FROM THE MIDWEST

1 ISLES BUN & COFFEE, MINNEAPOLIS, MN

Since they open daily at 6:30 a.m., the morning crew gets in nice and early to roll, sugar, and bake the first batches of their signature buns.

2 GOODY GOODY, ST. LOUIS, MO

A waitress at Goody Goody with plates of their fried chicken and waffles, slinger omelets, and other morning specialties.

3 THE BACHELOR FARMER, MINNEAPOLIS, MN

This charming restaurant is known for its sumptuous brunch cart, stocked with chilled Champagne and dessert.

4 LOU MITCHELL'S, CHICAGO, IL

At this local joint, many of the employees have been working the room for decades. Case in point: Donna Fenton, who is in her eighties and has been plying her trade for more than 27 years.

5 HAPPY GILLIS CAFE AND HANGOUT, KANSAS CITY, MO

The very sunny Green Eggs & Ham from Happy Gillis, a sweet cafe with a loyal clientele.

6 THE BRISTOL, CHICAGO, IL

Chef Chris Pandel's Hangover Breakfast, a bowl filled with house-made noodles, broth, and fixings—definitely designed to cure what ails you!

CHAPTER THREE

THE

SOUTH

RALEIGH, NC

JOULE **THE BLT DELUXE** 110

CHARLESTON, SC

HOMINY GRILL **SHRIMP AND GRITS** 115

MEMPHIS, TN

ELWOOD'S SHACK
**BARBECUED BRISKET BREAKFAST
BURRITO** 117

BIRMINGHAM, AL

ALABAMA BISCUIT COMPANY
**SPELT BISCUITS WITH GOAT CHEESE,
PECAN BUTTER, AND HONEY** 120

OXFORD, MS

HONEY BEE BAKERY
BRIOCHE CINNAMON BUNS 122

BIG BAD BREAKFAST
SOUTHWESTERN SKILLET 127

NEW ORLEANS, LA

LI'L DIZZY'S **CREOLE FILE GUMBO** 128

THE OLD COFFEEPOT **CALAS CAKES** 132

DONG PHUONG
PHO BO (BEEF NOODLE SOUP) 135

HOUSTON, TX

BLACKSMITH
**BISCUITS WITH COUNTRY HAM AND
REDEYE GRAVY** 139

SAN ANTONIO, TX

EL MILAGRITO CAFÉ **CHALUPA ROBERT** ... 141

AUSTIN, TX

TACODELI **MIGAS TACOS** 144

LAMBERT'S **FRITO PIE** 148

MIAMI, FL

HOME OF LEE SCHRAGER
**MARLENE SCHRAGER'S GERMAN
BREAKFAST (FOR DINNER)** 153

FOAR
BACON, EGG, AND CHEESE "PACO" 154

VERSAILLES
TORTILLA DE PAPAS (POTATO OMELET)
.... 157

BUENA VISTA DELI **QUICHE LORRAINE** 159

PANTHER COFFEE AND CINDY KRUSE'S
BAKED GOODS
MORNING GLORY MUFFINS 160

EATING HOUSE
**CUBAN BREAD TORREJAS WITH GUAVA
SYRUP, CREAM CHEESE, AND MARIA
COOKIE SUGAR** 164

27 RESTAURANT
**MALAWACH (YEMENITE FRIED
BREAD)** 167

HOME OF CHEF INGRID HOFFMANN
**YUCA BUNS AND OATMEAL
BREAKFAST SHAKE** 170

THE HEART OF BREAKFAST COUNTRY

When you think of those classic morning comfort foods—grits, biscuits, gravy, and bacon—no other region represents as winningly as the one below the Mason-Dixon line. Our Southern morning-eating tour took us to cities like Raleigh, where James Beard award–winning chef Ashley Christensen not only blew us away with her own food, but turned us on to Mecca, a decades-old classic that stands for all that is right and good.

At Elwood's Shack in Memphis, we found a career-changing restaurateur piling his barbecue into a breakfast burrito. Birmingham revealed a biscuit maker using ancient-grain flour. In Oxford, John Currence made morning-hours magic in a skillet—but not before we'd eaten pulled pork on pillowy hamburger buns practically before we'd uttered our first words of the day. In New Orleans, the beignets, gumbo, and a local rice fritter we'd never even heard of exceeded our expectations.

Then there's Lee's beloved hometown of Miami, which is a melting-pot culture owing a debt of gratitude to its huge Latin American population. We can think of few more quintessentially Miami experiences than lining up at the outside window for a pastry served with a generous helping of political discussion. On the other end of the spectrum, Miami's sense of adventurous fun is on display at places like 27 Restaurant, where the city's hippest bar impresarios are now putting out food that fuses local ethnic traditions into something entirely new. Like everything else in Miami, every day is full of surprises; thank goodness there's always great food to count on.

THE BLT DELUXE

....*Serves 4*

As the owner of multiple Raleigh establishments, Ashley Christensen is the town's reigning restaurateur. In the morning, locals head over to Joule, her high-concept coffee shop–cum-restaurant with one of the most ambitious java programs in the country; think a coffee sommelier, iced coffee made with coffee ice cubes, and more ways to brew a cup than there are biscuit recipes. Her weekend brunch offerings include this awe-inspiring BLT, stacked high with juicy tomato slices and crisp strips of bacon. The crowning glory is the malt aïoli, a tangy dressing that sends your taste buds to a British fish and chips shop with every bite.

For the Malt Aïoli

2 tablespoons **malt vinegar** (see Cook's Note)

1 teaspoon **Dijon mustard**

1 large **egg** plus 1 large pasteurized **egg yolk**

¾ cup **canola oil**

¼ teaspoon **salt**

¼ teaspoon **freshly ground black pepper**

For the Sandwiches

2 ripe **avocadoes**, sliced

2 tablespoons **fresh lemon juice**

Kosher salt and **freshly ground black pepper** to taste

4 **heirloom tomatoes**, thickly sliced

1 tablespoon **extra-virgin olive oil**

8 slices **sourdough bread**, lightly toasted

2 small heads of **butter lettuce**, leaves washed and dried well in a salad spinner

20 pieces **cooked bacon**

recipe continues

1 ***Make the malt aïoli:*** In the small bowl of a food processor, combine the vinegar, mustard, whole egg, and egg yolk and process until blended. With the motor running, slowly drizzle in the oil until a thick mayonnaise is formed. Season with the salt and pepper and chill for up to 2 days.

2 ***Make the sandwiches:*** Toss the avocadoes with the lemon juice and season with salt and pepper. Season the tomatoes with additional salt and pepper and drizzle with the olive oil.

3 Slather 1 tablespoon of the aïoli on one side of each piece of toast. Layer each of 4 slices of bread with a quarter of the avocadoes, a quarter of the lettuce leaves, 3 tomato slices, and 5 pieces of bacon. Carefully arrange the other slice of bread on top, press gently, and secure with sandwich toothpicks, which will be very helpful in keeping the sandwich together as you attempt to slice it. Using a serrated knife, carefully cut each sandwich in half on the bias. Serve with napkins . . . lots of napkins.

TIP

HOW TO PICK AN AVOCADO

HAAS AVOCADOES, easily identifiable by their bumpy moss-green skin, are reliably the creamiest and most delicious ones available. To select, look for smooth avocados, and err on the side of firm—once they over-ripen, they're hard to slice (which is important for this recipe) and can become slightly sour. Buy your avocadoes one day away from ripe—the skin will be dark brown and the fruit will still resist when pressed with your finger. Ripen on the counter or, to accelerate the process, place in a brown paper bag, which starves them of oxygen but still allows them to breathe through the porous material. Use ripe avocados within a day, or pop them in the fridge for an extra day or two.

The coffee counter at Joule

Mecca, Raleigh, NC

Back when Raleigh was one of the premier shopping
hubs of the South, there was one place to be for a ladies'
lunch or pretheater dinner: Mecca. "Women dressed up;
men wore ties; heck, even *he* had to dress up," said Floye
Dombalis, eighty-three, waving from her perch behind
the mechanical register as her son, Paul, waved from the
back. "Politicians knew they had to come to Mecca to
be seen," said Floye, pulling open a cabinet to show off
pictures of herself with various Supreme Court justices,
local politicians—and even Colonel Sanders. "Of course
he came here," joked Floye. "Where else do you think he
learned how to make fried chicken?" At the bar, a waitress
mixed pitcher after pitcher of sweet tea for lunch. Scratch
biscuits cooled on the pass-through, and the smell of bacon
wafted through the dining room. Back in the kitchen, Paul,
handsome at sixty-one and dressed in a blue shirt and
simple half apron, stood cracking eggs by hand into a white
porcelain bowl. A giant butcher's slab—installed for the
restaurant's opening in 1930 and marked with decades of
deep knife cuts—remains in use to this day.

   During Raleigh's heyday young Paul would come to
work with his grandfather, who allowed him to crank the
manual operator that hoisted food up from the storage
basement. Hard-pressed to imagine something he'd want
to do more, he stayed on through good times and bad.
Through decades of blight, Mecca held on. Downtown
Raleigh is now in the midst of a revival, with sparkling high-
rises and new bars, and restaurants seemingly popping up
every month. Paul said he's planning on working until the
restaurant's hundredth anniversary in 2030, at which point
he hopes his own son will have taken it over. "The moral of
the story," he said with a twinkle in his eye, "is never do too
good a job. Look where it gets you."

TOP TO BOTTOM: The matriarch of Mecca,
Floye Dombalis; a classic breakfast at
Mecca; keeper of the flame Paul Dombalis

SHRIMP AND GRITS

Serves 4

When everyone tells you to go to one place for one dish, you don't ask questions: you just get in the car and drive. That was the case with the shrimp and grits at Hominy Grill. An ingredient introduced to Southern cooking by Native Americans, grits are often referred to as hominy in Charleston, where they're practically the city's official sustenance. Hominy Grill chef Robert Stehling relies on top-quality products, coaxing flavor out of each one.

For the Grits

1 cup **stone-ground grits,** such as Anson Mills

1 teaspoon **salt,** plus more to taste

¾ cup grated **sharp Cheddar cheese**

¼ cup finely grated **Parmigiano-Reggiano cheese**

3 tablespoons **unsalted butter**

½ teaspoon **freshly ground black pepper,** plus more to taste

½ teaspoon **vinegar-based hot sauce,** such as Tabasco, plus more to taste

For the Shrimp

3 slices **bacon,** chopped

Peanut oil, if needed

1 pound large (16–20 count) **shrimp,** cleaned and peeled (see Cook's Note)

2 tablespoons **all-purpose flour**

4 ounces **button mushrooms,** thinly sliced (1¼ cups)

1 large **garlic clove,** minced

½ teaspoon **vinegar-based hot sauce,** such as Tabasco

2 teaspoons **fresh lemon juice**

2 **scallions** (white and green parts), thinly sliced, plus more for garnish

recipe continues

1 ***Cook the grits:*** In a medium saucepan, bring 4½ cups water to a boil. Whisk in the grits and salt, reduce the heat to low, and cook, uncovered, stirring occasionally, until the grits are thickened, 35 to 40 minutes. Remove from the heat and stir in the cheeses, butter, pepper, and hot sauce. Season with additional hot sauce, salt, and pepper, if desired.

2 ***Cook the bacon and shrimp:*** In a medium skillet over low heat, cook the bacon, stirring occasionally, until crisp. Drain on paper towels, reserving the bacon fat and adding peanut oil if necessary so you have 1½ to 2 tablespoons fat.

3 Toss the shrimp with the flour until lightly coated, shaking off any excess. In the skillet with the reserved fat, cook the shrimp over medium-high heat until they begin to turn pink, 1 minute or less. Add the mushrooms and bacon and cook 1 additional minute. Add the garlic and cook, stirring, for 30 seconds (do not let the garlic brown). Stir in the hot sauce, lemon juice, and scallions and remove from the heat. Divide the grits among 4 shallow bowls and top with the shrimp mixture. Garnish with additional scallions.

--- **COOK'S NOTE** ---

Since this entire dish cooks in a short time, make sure everything is prepared in advance.

BARBECUED BRISKET BREAKFAST BURRITO

Serves 2

In the shadow of a giant home-improvement store sits this funky shack run by Tim Bednarski, a former chain-restaurant executive who dreamed of a smaller, more delicious life. It's not unusual to find a line of people waiting to order a hearty first meal of the day, ideally to be eaten under one of the umbrella-topped picnic tables outside. This breakfast burrito, featuring highly seasoned potatoes and a sweet-smoky barbecue sauce, is a mouthful; if you can't finish it all in one sitting, it makes a mean lunch.

1 small **Yukon Gold potato,** cubed (⅔ cup)

1 teaspoon **all-purpose seasoning,** such as Accent

2 tablespoons **canola oil,** plus more for frying eggs

1 medium **onion,** sliced (1 cup)

1 small **tomato,** diced (¼ cup)

6 ounces shredded **smoked beef brisket** or pastrami

4 **eggs**

4 slices **Cheddar cheese**

2 12-inch **flour tortillas**

¼ cup **bottled barbecue sauce**

1 In a small saucepan, cover the potatoes with cold water, bring to a boil, and boil until softened but not breaking apart, 8 minutes. Drain, transfer to a bowl, and cool for 10 minutes. Toss with the all-purpose seasoning.

2 Meanwhile, in a large skillet heat the oil over medium-low heat. Add the onion and cook, barely stirring, until the onion caramelizes, 20 minutes. Add the cooked potato cubes, tomato, and brisket, and mix until warmed through, 4 to 5 minutes.

3 In another pan, scramble the eggs (see page 231 for instructions). Using tongs, carefully warm the tortillas over a stovetop flame, 10 seconds per side.

4 Place each tortilla on an individual serving plate. Divide the mixture from the skillet among the 2 tortillas. Top each mound with 2 slices of Cheddar cheese and half of the scrambled eggs. Drizzle half the barbecue sauce on each tortilla, roll up and serve.

Bryant's Breakfast, Memphis, TN

Phil Bryant has a story he feels illustrates the appeal of his Memphis institution to a T. "There was a famous trial going on in town, and one morning I realized that the prosecutor, judge, accuser, defendant, and some jury members were all in line at the same time," he said from behind the narrow counter as employees maneuvered around one another with the wordless, instinctual precision of a military submarine crew.

Originally opened in 1968 as a barbecue joint by his parents, Jimmy and Jane, Bryant's moved to its current location in 1977, where it quickly became famous for its from-scratch breakfasts. "My dad came here from Mississippi and all he owned was a sack of potatoes," said Phil as he stood near eight steaming coffeepots, peeking inside a foam clamshell container to quality-check an outgoing order. "He drilled the idea of good service into me, and it's something I try to never forget." Bryant's prides itself on its longtime staff; its come-one, come-all appeal; and, perhaps most of all, its fluffy, mile-high biscuits, which get slathered with butter and sorghum while still warm.

"How you start your day is how your day will end up," said Phil. "Getting something good that sticks with you is why people are here at 5:15 a.m., waiting for us to open." We had the feeling Phil's hospitality was equally important, something we confirmed as we headed to the parking lot. Phil rushed out and pressed a jar of sorghum into our hands. "Wanted to give you something else sticky," he said with a smile.

TOP: A high-wattage smile from behind the counter at Bryant's
BOTTOM: Second-generation owner Phil Bryant

SPELT BISCUITS

WITH GOAT CHEESE, PECANS, AND HONEY .... *Makes 12 biscuits*

In a part of the country where delicious biscuits are plentiful, the ones at the Alabama Biscuit Company stand out. Entrepreneur Jonathan Burch—an autodidact who taught himself how to cook by working his way through *Frank Stitt's Southern Table*, among others—opened the business to feed his parallel interests: cooking and healthy eating. Instead of White Lily flour Burch uses sprouted spelt flour, which adds nutty whole-grain goodness without sacrificing the levity that's non-negotiable here. Though Burch offers a variety of great toppings, we loved the simplicity of goat cheese, toasted pecans, and a drizzle of honey.

1 Preheat the oven to 450°F. In a medium bowl, whisk the flour, baking powder, and salt. Using a pastry blender or two chilled knives, cut in the butter until just incorporated (or pulse in a food processor until just combined). Drizzle in the buttermilk and stir until combined, being careful not to overmix.

2 On a floured work surface, form the dough into a 12-inch round, dusting with additional flour if necessary. Using a 3-inch cutter, cut out biscuits in one firm up-and-down motion (avoid twisting) and transfer to a baking sheet, leaving 3 inches between biscuits. Gently gather the scraps, pat them together, and cut out additional biscuits. Bake until fluffy and browned, 10 minutes.

3 In a medium bowl, whisk the goat cheese and yogurt until smooth Split the biscuits, dollop with the goat cheese mixture, drizzle with honey, and top with pecans.

1 pound (3⅔ cups) sprouted **spelt flour,** preferably To Your Health brand (see Cook's Note), plus more for the work surface

3½ teaspoons **aluminum-free baking powder**

1 teaspoon **fine sea salt**

12 tablespoons (1½ sticks) **unsalted butter,** cubed and chilled

1 cup **buttermilk,** preferably fuller-fat

8 ounces **goat cheese,** softened

1 cup **Greek yogurt**

Honey, for drizzling

1½ cups **pecan halves,** toasted, for garnish

--- **COOK'S NOTE** ---

Sprouting the flour is said to release its nutrients, making them easier to absorb. To Your Health flours are available at www.healthyflour.com; other brands are readily available at health food stores and Whole Foods.

BRIOCHE CINNAMON BUNS

.... *Makes 16 buns*

Small towns are lucky to have talented bakers like Shannon Adams, who makes absolutely every last item in the pastry case from scratch every day. Honey Bee is a family business; her mother—who also taught her to bake—is her business partner, and her brother, Sean, does the savory cooking. But to our minds the can't-miss pick is one of Shannon's thickly frosted cinnamon buns, made with a foolproof brioche dough that anyone can nail at home on the first try. There's a lot of yeast in the dough, which lends a fermented, almost bourbon-like flavor boost. Icing while the buns are still slightly warm helps the sugary white topping spread evenly.

For the Sponge

2 large **egg whites** (you should have ¼ cup)
¾ teaspoon **sugar**
1½ cups **bread flour**
2 teaspoons **instant or active dry yeast**

For the Dough

4 large **egg yolks**
1½ cups **bread flour,** plus more for rolling the dough
3 tablespoons **sugar**
1 teaspoon **kosher salt**
2 sticks (½ pound) **unsalted butter,** cubed,
    at room temperature
6 tablespoons **granulated sugar**
1 tablespoon **cinnamon**
Cooking spray

recipe continues

For the Icing

¼ cup **heavy cream**
¼ cup **half-and-half**
3½ cups **confectioners' sugar**
Pinch of **kosher salt**

1 ***Make the sponge:*** In a large mixing bowl, whisk the egg whites, ¾ cup water, and the sugar. Sprinkle the bread flour and yeast on top of the wet ingredients, and, using a wooden spoon, fold in until the ingredients come together. (Mixture will be goopy.) Cover with a clean kitchen towel and let sit in a warm place until the sponge begins to bubble and come alive, from 30 minutes to 2 hours.

2 ***Make the dough:*** Place the sponge in the bowl of a stand mixer fitted with the hook attachment. Add the egg yolks on top of the sponge. Mix on low speed until the yolks are incorporated, 3 minutes. Sprinkle the bread flour, sugar, and salt on top of the mixture and mix on low until incorporated, 2 minutes. Turn off the mixer and let the dough rest for 12 minutes. Turn the mixer on low and add the cubed butter by the tablespoon until well incorporated, continuing to mix 1 additional minute. Cover with a kitchen towel and refrigerate until the dough rises and doubles in size, 1 to 1½ hours. Punch down the dough; it should be cold to the touch (if the dough is not yet cool, chill it a little longer).

Self-taught pastry wiz and Honey Bee co-owner Shannon Adams icing her cinnamon buns

3 Divide the dough in half; each piece should weigh about 1 pound. Using a lightly floured rolling pin, roll out one section of dough on a floured surface into a 10 × 12-inch rectangle. Sprinkle evenly with 3 tablespoons of the sugar and ½ tablespoon of the cinnamon. Roll the dough lengthwise like a jelly roll and pinch the seams together to form a solid cylinder. Use a bench scraper to slice the dough in half, then in half again, then one more time to yield 8 individual rolls. Repeat with the other section of dough.

4 Spray a 9-inch round cake pan with cooking spray. Place 1 roll in the center and nestle the remaining rolls around it in a concentric circle. Lightly cover with a clean kitchen towel. Repeat with the remaining dough in a second pan. Let the dough rise until doubled in size (approximately the height of the pan itself), 45 minutes to 1 hour.

5 While the dough finishes rising, preheat the oven to 450°F. Once the dough has doubled, cover each pan securely with aluminum foil. Bake for 10 minutes, then reduce the heat to 350°F and continue baking for 15 minutes, checking the internal temperature with an instant-read thermometer to ensure the dough reaches 200°F (the rolls will be pale). If not done, uncover and cook for an additional 5 minutes. Remove from the oven and set on a wire rack until just slightly warm. Remove the rolls from the pan and set on a baking sheet lined with a wire rack.

6 ***Make the icing:*** In a stand mixer fitted with the paddle attachment, combine the heavy cream, half-and-half, confectioners' sugar, and salt and beat on low speed for 2 minutes until you get a thick, spreadable icing. Ice the rolls generously, allowing some icing to fall over the sides if you like.

SOUTHWESTERN SKILLET .... *Serves 4*

On weekends, lines are long to get into Oxford chef John Currence's breakfast haven, where all things Southern and delicious come together on the plate. Our favorite dish at BBB was this spicy, chili-laced skillet topped with corn tortilla strips, which are a breeze to make.

1 Make the hash: Steam the potato cubes until soft but not breaking apart, 10 minutes. Transfer to a baking sheet to cool for 10 minutes. In a large bowl combine all the spices. Toss the potato cubes in the spice mixture to evenly coat. Heat a large (10- to 12-inch) cast-iron skillet over medium-high heat. Put the oil in the skillet and then the potatoes; cook for 15 minutes, stirring occasionally, until browned and crisped. Transfer to a bowl and reserve. Wipe out the skillet with a paper towel and set aside.

2 Fry the tortillas: Fill a medium saucepan halfway with corn oil and heat to 350°F. Stack the tortillas on top of one another and slice into thin strips. Drop the strips into the oil in batches and fry until crisp, 1 to 2 minutes, allowing the oil to reheat for a minute between batches. Drain on paper towels and season with salt to taste.

3 Make the skillet: Preheat the oven to 450°F. In the reserved skillet over medium-high heat, sauté the clarified butter, onion, and jalapeños for 1 minute. Add the corn, potato hash, and grilled chicken and sauté for another minute, stirring to combine. Add the eggs and scramble. When the eggs are set, top with the cheese and place in the oven to melt, 3 minutes. Remove from the oven, slice, and serve, topping with the salsa and crispy tortilla strips. Garnish with scallions and fresh flat-leaf parsley.

For the Potato Hash

4 medium **potatoes** (¾ pound), unpeeled, cubed

2 tablespoons **chili powder**

1 tablespoon **ancho chile powder**

2 tablespoons **paprika**

1 tablespoon **salt**

1 tablespoon **freshly ground black pepper**

1½ tablespoons **ground cumin**

1 tablespoon **ground coriander**

1½ teaspoons **cayenne pepper**

3 tablespoons **canola oil**

For the Skillet

Corn oil, for frying

4 **corn tortillas** (or 2 cups crumbled corn tortilla chips)

Kosher salt

¼ cup **clarified butter** (see page 212)

1 small **onion,** chopped (½ cup)

2 **jalapeño peppers,** seeded and thinly sliced

1 cup **corn kernels,** fresh or frozen, thawed

10 ounces **grilled chicken,** chopped

8 large **eggs,** beaten

2 cups shredded **Cheddar cheese**

1 cup **salsa,** or more to taste

¼ cup sliced **scallions** (white and green parts), for garnish

Chopped **fresh flat-leaf parsley,** for garnish

CREOLE FILE GUMBO

Serves 6 to 8

We arrived for breakfast at Li'l Dizzy's just as churches in the Seventh Ward—and all over town—were letting out, releasing hungry worshipers eager to reward their devotion with a visit to the restaurant's famed morning buffet. At the host podium stood Wayne Baquet, a New Orleans hospitality legend whose family has owned restaurants in town for decades. When asked why his name sounded familiar, he answered coolly: "You may have heard of my brother, Dean? He's the editor of a little paper called the *New York Times*." Wayne ran the room like a benevolent dictator, rearranging tables for family groups or inching out a two-top to accommodate a favorite patron's ample girth. Though also known for one of the best versions of fried chicken in town, Li'l Dizzy's Creole file gumbo captivated us with its salty, porky, seafood-packed goodness. Defying conventional wisdom, some of the seafood is cooked for a long time, which we didn't mind at all here. It's the perfect version of a dish more generally associated with dinner than breakfast. We stand corrected.

⅓ cup **canola oil**

10 ounces **smoked ham,** cubed (2 cups)

1 medium **onion,** chopped (1 cup)

¾ pound **bone-in chicken thighs,** hacked into 2-inch pieces with a meat cleaver (or ask your butcher to do it)

10 ounces **smoked sausage,** sliced (2 cups)

¼ pound **hot sausage,** sliced (1 cup)

2 tablespoons chopped **garlic**

4 **scallions** (green and white parts), chopped (½ cup)

½ small **green bell pepper,** seeded and chopped (½ cup)

1 teaspoon **dried thyme leaves**

recipe continues

1 In a heavy 8-quart stockpot, heat the oil over medium-high heat. Add the ham and cook, stirring, until browned, 5 minutes. Add the onion and cook, stirring, until translucent, 5 minutes. Add the chicken pieces and smoked and hot sausage and cook, stirring, until golden, 6 to 7 minutes.

2 Add the garlic, scallions, bell pepper, thyme, and bay leaves and cook, stirring, for 5 minutes. Sprinkle in the flour and cook, stirring until incorporated, 2 minutes. Add 5 cups water, stir the pot vigorously, and bring the liquid to a simmer. Add the crabmeat and cook until the gumbo thickens, 45 minutes.

3 Add the oysters and shrimp and cook an additional 5 minutes. Turn off the heat, add the gumbo file powder, and stir well. Season with additional gumbo file, salt, and pepper to taste. Serve over cooked rice.

3 **bay leaves**
2½ tablespoons **all-purpose flour**
2 cups **fresh crabmeat,** picked through
1 cup **shucked oysters**
¾ pound **peeled shrimp**
1 tablespoon **gumbo file powder,** plus more to taste (see Cook's Note)
Kosher salt and freshly ground pepper to taste
Cooked rice, for serving

—————— **COOK'S NOTE** ——————

Made from the ground leaves of the sassafras tree, gumbo file powder is essential here. Not only does it add the necessary thickness — replacing a traditional roux — it gives a distinctive, mildly herbal flavor to this iconic dish.

TOP RIGHT: Owner Wayne Baquet

BOTTOM RIGHT: Three satisfied customers

BOTTOM LEFT: A portrait of Miles Davis oversees breakfast at Lil' Dizzy's

CALAS CAKES

......Makes 16 fritters

New Orleans food expert Poppy Tooker remembers the first time she prepared calas (pronounced ka-LAH)—puffy, sweet little pillows of flour-bound cooked rice she considers a personal obsession—at a local food fair about twenty-five years ago. "A man came up to me with tears in his eyes and told me they tasted just like his long-gone mother's version," says Tooker. "So clearly, calas are a food that can make a grown man cry . . . and bring someone back from the grave." Originally brought over to New Orleans by rice-growing African slaves, calas were prepared and sold by female vendors on Sunday, their traditional day off. They'd set up shop on the street, chanting, "Belle calas" (beautiful calas) as the scent of fresh, hot fritters permeated the air.

For the "Calas Ladies," fritter sales were about more than making extra money: New Orleans law dictated that if slaves could earn their price, they could buy back their freedom. "This is a dish that has far greater historical significance than a beignet," says Tooker. Calas Ladies disappeared after World War II, and with them a beloved tradition seemed on the verge of dying. But then Tooker championed the cause, publishing recipes both traditional and updated that led to a local revival. Soon she began seeing both savory and sweet versions on menus at restaurants like Herbsaint and Bayona. But for the classic sweet calas, you can still go to the Old Coffeepot, a 122-year-old restaurant in the French Quarter known for its rich breakfasts.

recipe continues

CLOCKWISE FROM LEFT: The finished dish; a calas cake, formed and ready for frying; calas cakes in the fryer

1 In a large bowl whisk the eggs, ½ cup water, the granulated sugar, cinnamon, and vanilla until foamy. Add the rice and stir to coat it well, then combine the flour and baking powder and sift them into the bowl and stir until just moistened (dough will be wet and slightly sticky). Moisten your hands with cold water or oil and form balls out of the batter, 3 tablespoons at a time, to make 16 balls.

2 Fill a large pot halfway with oil and heat to 350°F. Fry in batches, turning a few times to cook evenly, until the calas are golden and crisp, 7 to 8 minutes. Allow the oil to return to temperature between batches. Drain on a paper towel–lined plate, cut in half while warm, sprinkle with confectioners' sugar, and serve immediately.

Canola or other neutral oil, for deep-frying
2 large **eggs**
¼ cup **granulated sugar**
2 teaspoons **cinnamon**
1 teaspoon **vanilla extract**
3 cups **cooked long-grain rice** (1 cup raw)
1½ cups **all-purpose flour**
2 teaspoons **baking powder**
Confectioners' sugar, for serving

COOK'S NOTE

Though some classic recipes call for an overnight, yeast-risen dough, the Old Coffeepot's calas are made with baking powder. Poppy Tooker approves: "Yeast is too much planning for me," she concludes. "This makes them an à la minute indulgence."

A view of the Big Easy

PHO BO (BEEF NOODLE SOUP) .... *Serves 8*

On a typical Sunday morning in Little Vietnam, Kevin Tran, his parents, and their staff waited for the first rush. Inside the compact kitchen, several women stockpiled metal compartments with fresh herbs, sprouts, cabbage, cucumbers, and carrots; a giant colander dripped, filled to the brim with opaque rice noodles. "It all starts now," said Tran, fortifying himself with an iced Vietnamese coffee. The first cars began pulling up to the family's cavernous restaurant, and Dông Phuong filled up with Sunday churchgoers.

One of several restaurants serving the large Vietnamese community here, Dông Phuong is especially known for its pho, which Americans know as an exotic dinner order but in Vietnam is almost always served for breakfast. Like countless others, Tran's parents immigrated to New Orleans from Vietnam in the mid-1970s, attracted to the similarly hot, humid climate and a coastal fishing culture that provided work for thousands. The restaurant they took over in 1981 quickly became known for authentic dishes.

Though his parents barely speak English, Kevin transitions effortlessly between Vietnamese and English, helping run the business. Long tables ordered countless noodle dishes, salads, meat entrées, and side dishes—but each table had at least one order of their beef pho, made glossy by a stock enriched by pounds and pounds of gelatinous bones. They topped the steaming bowls with the traditional accoutrements: fresh herbs, lime wedges, Thai chiles, fish sauce, and chili sauce—all washed down with fruit shakes and ice-cold Tiger beers. By the front door, men in ribbed white tanks and flip-flops, their arms adorned by nautical tattoos, awaited take-out orders while reading the local Vietnamese papers. "We make sure everyone comes out of here looking like this," said Kevin's dad, holding an imaginary swollen belly. "If they're not full, they stay."

recipe continues

For the Broth

1 very large **onion**, unpeeled, halved

5-inch length of **ginger**, unpeeled

7 pounds **beef soup bones** (a combination of marrow and other bones)

4 **star anise**

7 **whole cloves**

1 **cinnamon stick**

1 pound **beef brisket**, cut into chunks and tied securely in cheesecloth

1½ tablespoons **kosher salt**

¼ cup good-quality **fish sauce**

2-inch piece of **rock sugar**, or 2 tablespoons light brown sugar

For the Soup

Fish sauce, kosher salt, and sugar to taste

¾ pound **sirloin steak**

1½ pounds dried thin Thai **rice stick noodles**, or 2 pounds fresh

Leaves from ½ small bunch of **fresh Thai or regular basil**

Leaves from ½ small bunch of **fresh cilantro**

Leaves from ½ small bunch of **fresh mint**

Lime wedges

1 cup **bean sprouts**

15 **Thai bird chiles**, or 2 small jalapeño peppers, finely chopped

1 small **yellow onion**, very thinly sliced

1 **Make the broth** (ideally begin this the night before): Preheat the broiler to low. Arrange the onion and ginger on a baking sheet and broil, turning, until charred, 6 to 7 minutes per side; cool. Discard the charred onion and ginger skins. Meanwhile, in a 12-quart stockpot, cover the bones with cold water, bring to a boil, and boil for 5 minutes, then strain and rinse the bones in a large colander. Rinse the pot, return the bones to the pot, and cover with 7 quarts water. Bring to a boil, reduce the heat, and simmer, skimming for the first 10 minutes. Add the charred vegetables, the star anise, cloves, cinnamon stick, brisket, salt, fish sauce, and sugar and return to a boil, then reduce the heat and simmer until the meat is cooked, 1 hour.

2 Transfer the meat to a bowl and cover with 3 cups of water and ½ cup ice; when the meat is cool, strain, discarding the liquid, and refrigerate the meat. Continue cooking the broth until it darkens and reduces by one third, 1½ to 2 hours more. Pass the broth through a colander, discarding all solids. Chill the broth overnight, then skim and discard the solidified fat from the top.

3 **Assemble the soup:** Gently reheat the broth as you prepare the other ingredients; season the broth with fish sauce, salt, and sugar to taste. Freeze the sirloin for 15 minutes, then very thinly slice it against the grain. Soak the dried noodles according to package directions (making sure not to over-soak) until somewhat soft but still al dente, 15 minutes; drain. Arrange the basil, cilantro, mint, lime wedges, sprouts, and chiles on a serving tray.

4 Place about ¾ cup noodles in each bowl. Distribute the brisket, sirloin, and onion evenly among the bowls. Ladle a generous amount of broth over each bowl, shaking slightly to make sure the broth seeps between all the ingredients. Set out the tray of garnishes and serve immediately as the meat continues to cook.

Dông Phuong owner Kevin Tran

BISCUITS WITH COUNTRY HAM AND REDEYE GRAVY .... *Serves 8*

When he set out to create the ultimate coffee shop, Chris Shepherd—the award-winning chef of Underbelly—wasn't content to merely curate one of the country's best coffee programs. He also insisted on the kind of food his chef friends would want to eat before heading in to work for the day, like these biscuits with savory, coffee-laced redeye gravy and slivers of salty country ham. The dish may seem deceptively simple, but its layers of flavor start with a ham hock stock that simmers for hours, forming a soulful broth that adds subtle body and tons of flavor to the finished product.

1 ***Make the biscuits:*** Preheat the oven to 325°F. In a bowl using your hands or in a food processor, combine the flour, sugar, salt, and baking powder. Add the butter, pinching quickly with your fingers or pulsing in the processor until the butter is integrated but chunks are still visible. Add the buttermilk and mix with a spoon or pulse until just combined, making sure not to overmix. Gently press the dough into a small baking pan and let chill in the refrigerator, 10 minutes. Cut into 8 equal pieces, spread them out on a baking sheet, and bake until a toothpick comes out dry and the biscuits are light golden, 25 to 30 minutes. Cool on a baking rack.

2 ***Make the gravy:*** Heat a dry 10-inch cast-iron skillet over high heat for 3 to 4 minutes. In a bowl whisk the coffee, stock, cream, salt, and pepper. Pour the mixture into the hot skillet and bring to a boil, being careful the liquid does not overflow, and continue simmering vigorously until reduced by one third, 15 minutes (the gravy will be the consistency of a broth, thinner than a typical gravy).

recipe continues

For the Biscuits
(makes 8 biscuits)

2½ cups **all-purpose flour**

2 tablespoons **sugar**

1½ teaspoons **sea salt**

5 teaspoons **baking powder**

2 sticks (½ pound) chilled **unsalted butter,** cubed

1 cup cold **buttermilk**

For the Gravy

1 cup strong brewed **coffee**

1 cup **Ham Hock Stock** (recipe follows)

2 cups **heavy cream**

1 teaspoon **kosher salt**

1½ teaspoons **freshly ground black pepper**

6 ounces **country ham,** such as Benton's, or other ham of your choice, chopped

Vegetable oil, for frying the eggs

8 large **eggs**

4 **scallions** (white and green parts), finely chopped

3 *To serve:* Add the ham to the gravy and heat over medium heat. In a separate skillet, fry the eggs sunny-side up (see page 233). Place the bottom half of each biscuit in a bowl. Pour ⅓ cup of the gravy (making sure to incorporate the cooked ham bits) over the biscuit, top with an egg, and garnish with the scallions. Top everything off with the other biscuit half.

HAM HOCK STOCK .... *Makes 1½ quarts*

3 **ham hocks**
1 **celery stalk,** roughly chopped
1 **yellow onion,** chopped
1 large **carrot,** chopped

In a 4-quart saucepan combine the ham hocks, celery, onion, carrot, and 3 quarts water and bring to a boil, skimming if necessary. Lower the heat and simmer for 8 hours. Strain, discard the solids, and refrigerate for 8 hours and up to 24 hours. Remove and discard the solidified fat; the broth underneath will be jiggly and gelatinous.

COOK'S NOTE

Freeze the extra stock in ice cube trays, pop out, and store in Zilpoc bags. Use the stock cubes to thicken sauces, or as the base for any recipe that calls for good-quality stock.

Chef Chris Shepherd

CHALUPA ROBERT .... *Serves 4*

San Antonio is a flour tortilla kind of town; be it in a breakfast taco or a plate of huevos rancheros, corn just doesn't cut it here. At this spacious, super-casual restaurant, the tortillas are made by hand every morning by a staff of dedicated ladies who get to work before the sun rises. Many of those tortillas serve as the base for chalupas smothered in house-made refried beans (use the leftovers at dinnertime), savory picadillo (cooked, seasoned ground beef), a quick, spicy tomato sauce laced with chipotle, a sunny-side up egg, and avocado.

1 **Make the beans:** In a large stockpot, bring 3¾ quarts water, the beans, onion, and garlic to a boil; reduce the heat to medium and cook for 2½ hours, until the beans are tender. Add the salt, pepper, and cumin and stir. Drain the beans, saving 1 cup of the cooking water. Blend the cooked beans in a blender or food processor until smooth and set aside. In a large skillet over medium-low heat render the bacon, 5 to 6 minutes, then add the beans. Stir and warm through. Season with additional salt and pepper if needed. Cover to keep warm.

2 **Make the picadillo:** In a large skillet heat the oil over medium heat; add the onion, garlic, and bell pepper and cook until softened, 7 to 8 minutes. Add the ground beef and cook, breaking up the meat with a wooden spoon, until browned, 5 minutes. Add the potato, carrot, salt, and pepper and stir. Cover, reduce the heat to medium-low, and cook until the potato and carrot are tender, 15 minutes. Keep warm.

recipe continues

For the Refried Beans

1 pound **dried pinto beans**, soaked for 24 hours, drained, and rinsed

1 large **onion**, chopped (2 cups)

3 **garlic cloves**, chopped

1 tablespoon **kosher salt**, plus more to taste

1 tablespoon **freshly ground black pepper**, plus more to taste

1 teaspoon **ground cumin**

3 slices **bacon**, diced

For the Picadillo

2 tablespoons **vegetable oil**

1 medium **onion**, chopped (1½ cups)

1 **garlic clove**, minced

1 medium **green bell pepper**, chopped (¾ cup)

1 pound **extra-lean ground beef**

1 small **potato**, peeled and finely diced (1 cup)

1 medium **carrot**, diced (½ cup)

1 teaspoon **kosher salt**

¼ teaspoon **freshly ground black pepper**

3 Meanwhile, **make the red sauce:** In a medium skillet heat the oil over medium heat. Add the onion and cook until tender, 3 to 4 minutes. Add the tomatoes, chipotles in adobo sauce, and vinegar; bring to a boil, then reduce the heat and simmer until the mixture is thick and the tastes meld, 15 minutes. Cool slightly, then transfer to a blender and puree until smooth. Return the sauce to the skillet and keep warm over medium-low heat.

4 **Fry the tortillas:** Heat half an inch of oil in a skillet over medium-high heat until very hot, then fry the tortillas one by one until crisp, 20 to 30 seconds per side. Drain on paper towels and season with salt.

5 **Assemble and serve the chalupas:** Spread ¾ cup of the refried beans over a fried tortilla, then top with 1 cup of the picadillo and ¼ cup of the Cheddar (the cheese will melt from the warmth of the picadillo; if not, place the tortilla in a hot oven for 2 minutes). Repeat for the other tortillas. Fry the eggs sunny-side up (see page 233), season with salt and pepper, and slide them over the tortillas. Top each tortilla with ¾ cup of the red sauce, then garnish with a quarter of the avocado and cilantro leaves.

For the Red Sauce

1 tablespoon **canola oil**
½ small **onion,** finely chopped
1 28-ounce can whole **tomatoes** in juice
1 teaspoon chopped canned **chipotle in adobo sauce**
2 tablespoons **white vinegar**

4 flour **tortillas**
Canola oil for frying
1 cup grated **Cheddar cheese**
4 large **eggs**
Salt and **freshly ground black pepper** to taste
1 ripe **avocado,** mashed
Fresh cilantro leaves, for garnish

MIGAS TACOS .... *Serves 4*

Why is Austin such a breakfast taco town? "You have all kinds of people needing to eat at all different times," Roberto Espinosa told us at Tacodeli, a chain he started in 1999. Originally a school-teacher, Mexico–born Espinosa opened the first branch, and has watched his business grow every year. Tacos filled with bacon and potatoes are popular, but we loved this one, which is twice as local, seeing as it's inspired by another Tex-Mex dish—migas, a scramble of eggs, tortilla chips or strips, and toppings. We recreated the creamy Dona sauce—a top-secret recipe concocted years ago by a Tacodeli employee—as best we could.

For the Steak

1 pound **sirloin flap,** trimmed

1 tablespoon **olive oil**

1 tablespoon **paprika**

1½ teaspoons **kosher salt,** plus more for sprinkling

1 **lime wedge** (optional)

For the Migas

8 large **eggs**

¼ teaspoon **kosher salt**

1 tablespoon **unsalted butter**

½ cup chopped **tomato**

¼ cup chopped **onion**

2 small **jalapeño peppers,** seeded and finely chopped (¼ cup)

1 cup shredded **Monterey Jack cheese**

1 cup **tortilla chips,** crushed into bite-sized pieces

8 small **flour tortillas**

Salsa Roja (recipe follows)

Dona Sauce (recipe follows)

recipe continues

Tacos with all the fixings

1 **Cook the steak:** Preheat a cast-iron skillet or a griddle over medium-high heat to the point of smoking. Rub the sirloin with the olive oil, then season both sides of the meat with the paprika and salt. Place the sirloin in the skillet and cook until dark and seared, 3 to 4 minutes. Flip and cook until the inside is medium rare and the meat reads 130°F on an instant-read thermometer, 3 more minutes. Transfer the sirloin to a cutting board and let the meat rest for 5 minutes. Cut into 3/4-inch cubes and sprinkle with extra salt or a squeeze of lime, if desired.

2 **Make the migas:** In a medium bowl whisk the eggs with the salt until foamy. Heat a large skillet over medium-high heat, melt the butter, then add the eggs and cook, stirring, until scrambled and just set, 30 to 45 seconds (for soft-scrambled eggs, see page 231). Add the tomato, onion, jalapeños, cheese, and tortilla chips. Cook until the eggs are done but still moist, 1 to 2 more minutes.

3 To serve, briefly warm the tortillas in a clean skillet. Place 2 tortillas on each plate, divide the eggs among the 4 plates, top with the steak cubes, and serve with the salsa roja and Dona sauce.

SALSA ROJA .... *Makes 3 cups*

1 Heat a large cast-iron skillet over medium-high heat to the point of smoking (or heat an outdoor grill over high heat or preheat the broiler). Add the oil and swirl it around evenly in the skillet (or, if broiling, on a small baking sheet). Add the tomatoes, jalapeños, onion, and garlic and char the vegetables on all sides (the darker the vegetables get, the more flavor), 15 minutes total. Cool slightly.

2 Place the vegetables in a blender, removing and discarding the seeds from the chilies if you prefer a less spicy salsa. Add the cilantro, ½ cup water, and salt and blend thoroughly; season with more salt if necessary.

3 If the salsa is too thick, add water by the tablespoonful to reach desired consistency. If you prefer a chunkier salsa, pulse the salsa in a blender or food processor until you achieve the desired consistency. Salsa can be stored in the refrigerator in an airtight container for 3 days.

1 tablespoon **canola oil**
2 medium ripe **tomatoes**
3 **jalapeño peppers**
½ medium **onion,** sliced into ½-inch-thick rings
3 **garlic cloves**
½ cup **fresh cilantro leaves**
1½ teaspoons **kosher salt,** or more to taste

DONA SAUCE .... *Makes 1 cup*

Heat 1 tablespoon of the oil in a large skillet over medium-high heat. Add the jalapeños and garlic and cook until the peppers are blistered and the garlic is charred, 3 minutes per side. Transfer to a plate to cool. Place in a blender with the remaining oil and the salt and puree until smooth. Sauce will keep, refrigerated, in an airtight container for up to 1 week.

¼ cup **vegetable oil**
½ pound **jalapeño peppers,** trimmed, halved lengthwise, seeded, and deveined
4 **garlic cloves**
½ teaspoon **kosher salt,** or more to taste

FRITO PIE .... *Serves 4*

A favorite all over the Southwest, Frito pie comes in many variations—some even made by cutting open a single-serve bag of the addictive corn chips and filling it with chili and other fixings. We loved the brunchy version at Lambert's, a ten-year-old Austin barbecue restaurant featuring some of the best brisket in town. Chef Reid Guess layers his pie with the restaurant's signature meat, homemade queso—Austin's signature cheese sauce—a whole host of other cheeses, and a quick pico de gallo before topping it with a poached egg. When pierced, the yolk forms a sauce that coats the oven-crisped chips to perfection. Reserve the extra queso for topping just about everything.

1 **Make the pies:** Preheat the oven to 450°F. In a large bowl, toss together the brisket and cheeses. Add 3 cups of the chips and toss to incorporate. Divide the mixture between 4 individual baking dishes or ovenproof bowls. Drizzle ¼ cup of the queso and scatter ¼ cup of the remaining chips over each bowl. Arrange the dishes on a baking sheet and bake until the tops are browned, 10 minutes.

2 **Make the pico de gallo:** While the pies are baking, in a small bowl toss the onion, tomato, cilantro, jalapeño, vinegar, and salt for a pico de gallo–type condiment that can be used as a garnish or passed at the table.

3 **Finish the dish:** Poach the eggs (see page 231). Remove the pies from the oven and top with the eggs, sliced scallions, and sour cream, if using. Serve immediately.

recipe continues

For the Frito Pies

½ pound **barbecued beef brisket,** chopped
½ cup crumbled **queso fresco**
¼ cup crumbled **goat cheese**
¼ cup shredded **Cheddar cheese**
¼ cup shredded **Monterey Jack cheese**
4 cups **Fritos corn chips**
1 cup **Queso** (recipe follows)

For the Pico de Gallo

½ medium **onion,** finely chopped (½ cup)
1 small **tomato,** finely chopped (½ cup)
¼ cup **fresh cilantro leaves,** chopped
1 large **jalapeño pepper,** finely chopped (2 tablespoons)
1 tablespoon **white vinegar**
¼ teaspoon **kosher salt**

Vegetable oil and **unsalted butter,** for poaching the eggs
4 large **eggs**
4 **scallions** (white and green parts), finely sliced
½ cup **sour cream** (optional)

QUESO .... *Makes 3½ cups*

1 Preheat the broiler. Broil the poblanos on a baking sheet until their skin is charred and flesh is soft, turning 2 to 3 times, 12 to 14 minutes total. Transfer to a bowl, cover with plastic wrap, and let cool for 15 minutes. Peel the chiles, discarding the skin and seeds; finely chop them and set aside.

2 In a medium saucepan, melt the butter over medium heat. Add the onion and sauté until translucent, 4 minutes. Add the tomato and chiles and cook until slightly thickened, 3 to 4 minutes. Stir in the milk and bring to a boil, then add the cheeses, lower the heat to medium-low, and stir until the cheese is melted, 5 minutes. Remove from the heat. Queso will keep, refrigerated, for up to 1 week.

2 **poblano chiles**
1 tablespoon **unsalted butter**
½ medium **onion,** finely chopped
   (½ cup)
1 small **tomato,** finely chopped
   (½ cup)
½ cup **milk**
1 pound **yellow melting cheese,** such
   as American or Velveeta, shredded
2 cups shredded **Monterey**
   Jack cheese

COOK'S NOTE

The next time you're heading out for a feast at your local barbecue joint, make sure to order enough brisket to take home for this recipe!

TOP RIGHT: Lee with his parents, Marlene and Lee, and his dog, Charlie Brown

BOTTOM LEFT AND RIGHT: Lee making breakfast with his mother, Marlene

Lee's Miami

I've been in love with this town ever since I first visited my grandparents here at the age of ten. My family moved down here permanently a few years later. Other than the three years I spent at the Culinary Institute, I never left—and most probably never will. The eternal sunshine was what first got this Long Island boy hooked, but as an adult I am constantly seduced by the casual sophistication of the global population here, the sense of excitement and adventure that every day brings, the growing arts and culture scene—and, of course, the food.

Miami is where, as vice president of corporate communications and national events for Southern Wine & Spirits of America, I created both The Food Network and Cooking Channel South Beach and New York Wine and Food Festivals, which have grown into the world's most fabulous celebrations of eating and drinking. I've watched the local food scene and the festival grow side by side, and I consider many of the city's best chefs not only colleagues, but my personal friends. Nothing gives me more pleasure than patronizing their establishments—something I do every day that finds me in Miami. But if I really think about it, the most influential cook in my life has been my mother, Marlene, who lives in Fort Lauderdale.

MARLENE SCHRAGER'S GERMAN BREAKFAST (FOR DINNER) ....*Serves 4 to 6*

I can't quite remember when my mother first made her now-famous German breakfast (and exactly why it's "German"), but re-creating the dish with her recently in my new kitchen in Coral Gables, I marveled at how the smell of frying bacon, potatoes, onions, and peppers sent me right back to those days when she had to get a meal on the table in a hurry. Out of the fridge would come bacon, eggs, and vegetables, which she'd fry up with pre-cooked potatoes and onions for a one-skillet breakfast-for-dinner par excellence that my brothers, Richard and Howard, and I loved. Cooking this dish with her as an adult also gave me the opportunity to remember what's so elemental and incredible about food and family: how pulling together a few simple ingredients—and preparing them, even wordlessly, side by side—can be the basis for a beautiful, lifelong conversation.

½ pound **bacon**

1 jumbo **yellow onion,** chopped (3 cups)

1 large **red bell pepper,** seeded and diced (2 cups)

1 large **green bell pepper,** seeded and diced (2 cups)

1½ pounds **russet potatoes,** peeled, boiled, cooled, and diced

10 large **eggs,** lightly beaten

Salt and **freshly ground black pepper** to taste

1 In a very large (12- or 14-inch) skillet, cook the bacon over medium heat until crisp, 7 to 8 minutes. Transfer to a paper towel-lined plate and crumble when cool. Transfer the bacon fat to a bowl and reserve, returning 3 tablespoons to the skillet. Add the onion and both peppers and cook over medium-high heat, stirring occasionally, until the onion is browned and the peppers are softened, 11 to 12 minutes.

2 Add the potatoes and cook, stirring, until they begin to break up, 6 to 7 minutes. Push the mixture to one side of the skillet, add another tablespoon of bacon fat, and scramble the eggs until cooked. Add the bacon to the pan, stir together the entire mixture, season with salt and pepper, and serve immediately.

BACON, EGG, AND CHEESE "PACO"

Makes 6 pacos (pancake tacos)

Crispy bacon, melted cheese, and creamy eggs—all stuffed inside a soft, sweet pancake? This we had to try. We found the FOAR truck early on a Sunday morning, ready to serve their creative offerings to an "enwraptured" (you'll forgive the pun) audience. Unlike most pancakes, where the batter is gently mixed just until incorporated, these are worked a bit more to develop the gluten, resulting in a sturdier envelope for classic breakfast fillings.

1 Make the pancakes: Preheat the oven to 200°F. In a medium bowl, whisk together the flour, baking powder, sugar, and salt. In a large bowl, whisk together the milk, eggs, oil, and vanilla. Add the dry ingredients to the wet and mix for about 1 minute, until well incorporated. Heat a griddle or a nonstick skillet over medium-low heat and brush lightly with oil or butter. Ladle out ½ cup batter per pancake and cook until puffed and golden brown, 1 to 2 minutes per side. Transfer to a plate and keep warm in the oven, loosely covered, until ready to serve. Repeat with the remaining batter.

2 Make the fillings: On the same griddle or skillet, cook the bacon over medium-high heat until it begins to crisp, 2 to 3 minutes per side. Transfer to a paper towel–lined plate to drain and keep warm in the oven, so it does not get leathery. Remove and discard all but 2 tablespoons of the bacon grease, then cook the eggs over-easy (see page 233), seasoning them with a pinch of salt and pepper.

3 To serve, lay a pancake on a plate, place 2 bacon strips on half of the pancake, then top with an egg and a slice of cheese. Drizzle with maple syrup, fold over the other half, and serve immediately. Repeat with remaining ingredients.

For the Pancakes

1½ cups **all-purpose flour**

5 teaspoons **baking powder**

3 tablespoons **sugar**

1 teaspoon **kosher salt**

1½ cups **milk**

2 large **eggs**

3 tablespoons **canola oil**, plus more for the griddle

1 teaspoon **vanilla extract**

For the Fillings

12 slices **hardwood-smoked bacon**

6 large **eggs**

Kosher salt and **freshly ground black pepper** to taste

6 slices **American cheese**

Good-quality **maple syrup**, for drizzling

BOTTOM RIGHT: A special rack to mold the "taco pancakes"

BOTTOM LEFT: Rick Nassa, Evan Nassa, and Briana DeGenarro, the team behind the FOAR Truck

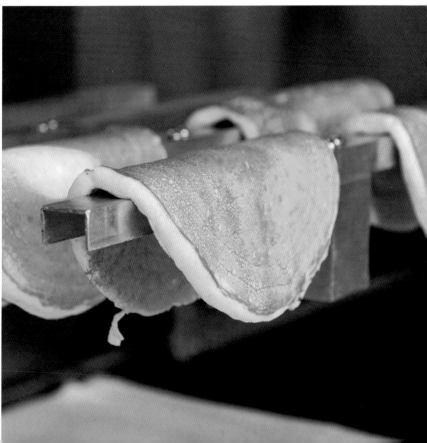

famously delicious Cuba

/VersaillesMiami   #LoveVersailles

TORTILLA DE PAPAS (POTATO OMELET) .... *Serves 8*

As simple as they come, this skillet potato-and-egg omelet is as good at room temperature as it is hot off the stove. It also makes great picnic food, eaten with your hands or sandwiched between two slices of bread for a double-carb treat. In Cuban homes, a tortilla like this one is a staple, made with just a few ingredients and requiring very little attention. At Versailles, it's a breakfast standard often ordered with a flaky *pastellito* (guava pastry) and a cup of milky coffee.

Vegetable oil, for frying
2 large **potatoes** (1 pound), peeled and cut into ½-inch cubes
¼ cup **olive oil**
6 large **eggs**
1 teaspoon **kosher salt**
½ teaspoon **freshly ground black pepper**
Chopped **fresh flat-leaf parsley,** for garnish

1 In a large deep skillet heat 2 inches of vegetable oil over medium-high heat. Carefully arrange the potatoes in the skillet in a single layer and reduce the heat to medium. Fry the potatoes until light golden brown, 8 to 9 minutes, stirring as needed to prevent sticking. Drain the potatoes on paper towels and let cool to room temperature. Reserve the cooking oil for another use, or discard.

2 In a nonstick skillet, heat the olive oil over medium heat. Scatter the cooked potatoes evenly to cover the bottom of the skillet. In a medium bowl, whisk the eggs with the salt and pepper, then pour the eggs evenly over the potatoes and cook without touching or moving them, until the bottom of the omelet is golden brown and set, 7 to 8 minutes.

3 Slide the omelet onto a plate slightly larger than the skillet, invert the skillet over the plate, and flip them both so the omelet lands back in the skillet. Cook the underside until golden, 4 to 5 minutes. Slide the omelet onto a plate, cut into wedges, garnish with parsley, and serve immediately or at room temperature.

Nicole Vals, a member of the family that owns Versailles

QUICHE LORRAINE ....*Serves 6 to 8*

When Lee lived in Miami's Design District, Cory Finot's super-casual spot was his breakfast destination of choice. Finot originally came from France to go to hotel school in 1999 and put down permanent roots, working all over town before opening Buena Vista in 2009. Though the food reads All-American comfort on the plate, the menu bears hallmarks of his Gallic roots. To wit: this quiche, to which Lee swears allegiance above all others.

1 **Make the crust:** In a food processor, combine the flour, sugar, and salt. Add the butter and pulse until the crust resembles coarse sand, 10 to 15 pulses. Add the water and pulse just until the dough comes together. Gather the dough into a ball, wrap it in plastic, and refrigerate for 20 minutes. Lightly butter a 12-inch-wide, 2-inch-deep pie dish; set aside.

2 On a lightly floured work surface, roll the dough into a 15-inch round using a large, floured rolling pin. Roll the dough over the rolling pin, then unroll it over the dish and adjust to fit. Trim the dough, leaving a 1-inch overhang. Fold the excess dough underneath, pressing to seal the 2 layers together. Using your fingers, crimp every inch around the perimeter. Refrigerate the dish for 30 minutes.

3 **Make the filling:** Preheat the oven to 325°F. In a bowl combine the cheese, ham, and prosciutto and scatter it evenly over the dough. In the same bowl, whisk the eggs, cream, milk, pepper, and nutmeg until combined. Pour the mixture evenly over the pie dish, shaking to ensure the liquid seeps to the bottom. Sprinkle the mozzarella cheese over the top. Bake, rotating midway through cooking, until light golden and the center sets, but is still soft, 80 to 90 minutes. Transfer to a rack for 10 minutes, cut into 6 wedges, and serve.

For the Crust

2 cups **all-purpose flour,** plus more for the work surface

2 tablespoons **sugar**

½ teaspoon **kosher salt**

10 tablespoons cold **unsalted butter,** cubed, plus more for greasing the dish

⅓ cup **ice water**

For the Filling

2½ cups shredded **Gruyère cheese**

2 cups finely diced thick-cut **ham**

4 thin slices of **prosciutto di parma,** chopped

4 large **eggs**

2 cups **heavy cream**

½ cup **whole milk**

½ teaspoon **freshly ground black pepper**

¼ teaspoon **grated nutmeg**

¾ cup shredded **mozzarella cheese**

BOTTOM RIGHT: Owner Cory Finot

MORNING GLORY MUFFINS .... *Makes 12 muffins*

Home to a growing number of art galleries and outdoor exhibitions, the Wynwood neighborhood is also where you'll find the flagship branch of the city's coolest coffee shop. All day there are artists, musicians, students, tourists, and unabashed coffee freaks waiting patiently in line for one of Panther's cold brews or impeccably sourced, single-bean coffees. Almost every morning, Cindy Kruse hand-delivers her scrumptious pastries; get there early or these morning muffins will most definitely be sold out. Good thing she gave us the recipe so you can sleep in and make them at home. Hers are made in larger professional paper muffin molds; we adapted the recipe to a standard 12-compartment muffin tin.

- 2 cups grated **carrots**
- 1 **apple,** peeled and grated
- 1 14-ounce can **crushed pineapple,** squeezed of excess liquid (1 cup drained)
- ½ cup shredded **sweetened coconut**
- 1 cup chopped **walnuts**
- ½ cup **golden raisins**
- 3 large **eggs**
- 1½ cups **sugar**
- 1½ cups **vegetable oil**
- 1½ teaspoons **vanilla extract**
- 2¼ cups **all-purpose flour**
- 2 teaspoons **cinnamon**
- 2 teaspoons **baking soda**
- 1 teaspoon **kosher salt**

recipe continues

1 Preheat the oven to 350°F. Line a 12-cup muffin tin with paper liners and set aside. In a medium bowl, combine the carrots, apple, pineapple, coconut, walnuts, and raisins. In a separate bowl, whisk the eggs, then whisk in the sugar until smooth. Whisk in the oil and vanilla.

2 In a third, large bowl, stir the flour, cinnamon, baking soda, and salt until well combined. Add the wet ingredients to the dry and stir just until all of the dry ingredients are moistened. Add the carrot-apple mixture to the batter and fold with a spatula until just combined. Divide the batter among the muffin liners and bake until a toothpick inserted in the center comes out clean, 30 minutes.

—— **COOK'S NOTE** ——

To freeze these muffins, wrap individually in plastic and freeze for up to 3 months.

TOP LEFT: A coffee tasting in progress

TOP RIGHT: Panther's famous cold brew coffee

CUBAN BREAD TORREJAS

WITH GUAVA SYRUP, CREAM CHEESE, AND MARIA COOKIE SUGAR......................................*Serves 4*

Inspired by staple ingredients easily found in the Cuban pantry, chef Giorgio Rapicavoli came up with this take on traditional Cuban French toast. Sweet guava paste, Iron Beer soda, condensed milk, and cream are combined into a duo of sauces that grace the lightly soaked and pan-toasted *torrejas*. The Maria cookies—similar to a petit-beurre cracker—get crushed with sugar for a crunchy topping.

For the Guava Syrup

1 pound **guava paste**
1 12-ounce can **Iron Beer** (or Dr Pepper)
Pinch of **kosher salt**

For the Cream Cheese Sauce

1 8-ounce package **cream cheese**, softened
½ cup **half-and-half**
¼ cup **sour cream**
¼ cup **sweetened condensed milk**
1 teaspoon **vanilla extract**
Pinch of **kosher salt**

For the Maria Cookie Sugar

8 **Maria cookies**, such as Gilda brand
¼ cup (packed) **light brown sugar**
Pinch of **kosher salt**

recipe continues

Chef Giorgio Rapicavoli

1 **Prepare the guava syrup:** Using a blender or food processor, blend the guava paste, Iron Beer, and salt until smooth, 30 seconds.

2 **Make the cream cheese sauce:** Combine the cream cheese, half-and-half, sour cream, sweetened condensed milk, vanilla, and salt in a blender or food processor and blend until smooth. Refrigerate the sauce until ready to use.

3 **Create the cookie sugar:** Place the cookies in a food processor and pulse until fine crumbs form. Add the brown sugar and salt and pulse until combined.

4 **Make the torrejas:** In a medium bowl, whisk the half-and-half, eggs, sugar, vanilla, and salt. When ready to cook, pour the custard mixture into a wide, shallow dish.

5 Preheat the oven to 225°F. Set a wire rack over a baking sheet. Dip the bread into the egg mixture, allowing it to soak for 30 seconds on each side. Transfer to the rack and drain for 1 to 2 minutes.

6 Melt 1 tablespoon of the butter on a griddle or 10-inch nonstick skillet. Cook 2 slices of bread at a time until golden brown, 2 to 3 minutes per side. Transfer to a plate, cover lightly with foil, and keep warm in the oven. Repeat with the remaining butter and bread.

7 For each serving, place 2 torrejas on a plate and top with ½ cup of the cream cheese sauce, drizzle with 2 tablespoons of the guava syrup, and sprinkle with 1 to 2 tablespoons of the Maria cookie sugar.

For the Torrejas

1 cup **half-and-half**
3 large **eggs**
2 tablespoons **sugar**
1 teaspoon **vanilla extract**
¼ teaspoon **salt**
1 loaf of stale **Cuban or Portuguese bread,** cut into 8 equal pieces
4 tablespoons (½ stick) **unsalted butter**

———— **COOK'S NOTE** ————

Several of the elements can be prepared in advance, making this a great wake-and-make brunch for company. The guava syrup will keep in the fridge in an airtight container for up to 3 weeks and the egg mixture for the torrejas can be made and refrigerated the night before you're ready to cook.

MALAWACH (YEMENITE FRIED BREAD) ....*Serves 4*

With an innate sense for what works in often fickle Miami, Gabriel Orta and Elad Zvi are building a mini-empire of cool. Spotting a craft-cocktail void in a mojito-soaked town, they opened Broken Shaker, as much a magnet for poolside hipsters as for chefs seeking a late-night respite from the line. Next came 27, a restaurant you might say appeals to the Yiddishe mamita in all of us. "Basically everyone in this town is either Latin or Jewish, so we decided to create a restaurant that combines those two things," says Zvi. Any given Sunday you'll find patrons tearing apart deliciously buttery malawach, similar to an Indian paratha and an homage to Zvi's Israeli heritage. 27's version is slightly less flaky than the one you'll find in Israel—which makes it much easier to pull off in a home kitchen—but no less delicious. In Israel malawach—one of several Yemenite breads that are beloved national comfort-food staples— is rarely made at home, but rather bought frozen and heated in an oiled pan. We think it's well worth the effort, but if you're pressed for time, seek out the frozen version at kosher markets and invest your time in the traditional condiments: *resek,* a grated-tomato puree, and *charif,* a fiery, pepper-laced sauce.

Co-owner Elad Zvi

1 **Make the malawach:** In the bowl of a stand mixer fitted with the hook attachment, combine the flour, 1½ cups water, and the salt and knead until a slightly sticky dough forms, 6 minutes (you can also knead by hand). Once the dough is formed, transfer to a flat, clean surface and knead by hand until smooth, 2 minutes, adding flour ¼ cup at a time, up to 1 cup, if necessary, if dough is too sticky. Divide the dough into 4 equal pieces, brush with about 2 tablespoons of the melted butter, cover with a damp cloth, and allow to rest for 25 minutes.

recipe continues

For the Malawach

4 cups **all-purpose flour,** plus more if necessary
1 tablespoon **kosher salt**
8 tablespoons (1 stick) **unsalted butter,** melted

2 Lay one piece of dough at a time on a clean work surface. Using your hands, stretch out the dough to a 9 × 11-inch rectangle, brush generously with some of the remaining melted butter, then fold the dough in half lengthwise 3 times until you have a 1 × 11-inch rope. Smooth the rope, tie two evenly spaced knots into the rope, and cover. Repeat with the rest of the dough, then cover and allow to rest for another 25 minutes.

3 Using your hands, flatten each piece of dough into a 9- or 10-inch circle. Heat a cast-iron pan until smoking and cook the dough until browned and lightly charred, 30 seconds to 1 minute on each side.

4 *Make the resek:* Use a box grater to grate the tomatoes into a medium bowl, discarding the skin. Whisk in the olive oil, paprika, cumin, salt, and pepper.

5 *Make the charif:* In a food processor, puree the cilantro, parsley, and olive oil into a fine paste, scraping down the sides of the bowl once or twice, 30 seconds. Add the tomato, bell and serrano chiles, garlic, red pepper flakes, lemon zest, and salt and pulse until combined, scraping down the bowl if necessary. Transfer to a serving bowl.

6 For each serving, arrange one malawach bread on a large plate or serving board. Mound ½ cup crumbled feta on the plate, drizzle with olive oil, and sprinkle with za'atar. Serve with a hard-boiled egg, resek, and charif.

─────── **COOK'S NOTE** ───────
Condiments can be prepared during the dough's resting times.

For the Resek

2 large, ripe **heirloom tomatoes,** halved
2 tablespoons **olive oil**
1 teaspoon **paprika**
1 teaspoon **ground cumin**
½ teaspoon **kosher salt**
½ teaspoon **freshly ground black pepper**

For the Charif

1 bunch of **fresh cilantro,** leaves and tender stems
¼ bunch of **fresh flat-leaf parsley,** leaves and tender stems
2 tablespoons **olive oil**
½ ripe **tomato,** diced
¼ **red bell pepper,** diced (¼ cup)
2 to 3 **serrano chiles,** seeds removed if desired, diced
2 **garlic cloves**
¾ teaspoon **dried red pepper flakes**
Grated zest of 1 small **lemon**
1 teaspoon **kosher salt**

2 cups crumbled **feta cheese**
Olive oil
Za'atar spice blend
(available from Worldspice.com or Kalustyans.com)
4 **hard-boiled eggs**

YUCA BUNS

AND OATMEAL BREAKFAST SHAKE .... *Makes 10 buns*

"I'm scared of these," Ingrid Hoffmann told us as she pulled a batch of piping hot *pan de yuca* from the oven in her beautiful studio kitchen, complete with killer views of Miami. We'd stopped by for a firsthand taste of Hoffmann's Colombian childhood, where a perfect Bogota day included a trip to a local bakery, Froufrou, for puffy, cheesy rolls we couldn't help comparing to oversized gougères. "I can't stop eating them," she told us, sharing them as much out of self-preservation as out of her natural generosity of spirit. Often Hoffmann serves them with this thick, cinnamon-laced *avena* (oatmeal) breakfast shake that's a meal in itself. Though you can make fresh oatmeal for the shake, it's also a perfectly good use for leftovers. You can also swap in almond, coconut, or another nut milk of your choice.

1 cup **tapioca starch** (also known
    as tapioca flour),
    plus extra for kneading
1 teaspoon **baking powder**
1¼ teaspoons **kosher salt**
¼ cup **heavy cream,** plus more
    as needed
2 cups finely grated **Oaxaca cheese**
    or other fresh white cheese,
    such as mozzarella
2 large **egg yolks**

1 Preheat the oven to 350°F. Line a baking sheet with parchment paper. In a large bowl, whisk together the tapioca starch, baking powder, and salt. Stir in the cheese, egg yolks, and cream. Once the dough forms a ball, turn it out onto a lightly floured work surface. Using your hands, knead the dough until smooth and not sticky. Add extra cream a tablespoon at a time if necessary to make the dough supple.

2 Divide the dough into 10 equal pieces and shape them into balls. Arrange them 1 inch apart on the prepared baking sheet and bake until pale golden, tender, and soft, 18 to 20 minutes. Serve hot.

OLD-FASHIONED OATMEAL (AVENA) BREAKFAST SMOOTHIES .... *Serves 4*

1 In a medium saucepan, bring the milk and oats to a rapid simmer over medium-high heat, stirring to prevent the oatmeal from sticking to the bottom of the pan. Reduce the heat to medium-low and cook, stirring constantly, until the oatmeal is thick, about 10 minutes. Remove from the heat, add the sugar and cinnamon to taste, and cool slightly, 10 to 15 minutes.

2 Refrigerate the oatmeal in a sealed container for at least 2 hours or overnight. Transfer the oatmeal to a blender, add the vanilla (if using), and puree until smooth, adding more milk for a thinner shake or ice cubes to chill further. Serve cold.

6 cups **milk,** plus more if needed
1 cup **old-fashioned rolled oats**
2 tablespoons **sugar,** or more to taste
Pinch of **cinnamon,** or more to taste
1 teaspoon **vanilla extract** (optional)

—— **COOK'S NOTE** ——
Make sure to prepare the oatmeal the night before you plan on making the smoothie.

Hoffmann often serves the avena and yuca
buns with a traditional "morning broth"
featuring a poached egg

1 2 CAFÉ DU MONDE, NEW ORLEANS, LA

A server at Café Du Monde with the establishment's signature offerings, beignets and chicory coffee.

3 4 PALACE, MIAMI, FL

Drag Brunch at Palace, where the food has to compete with beauties like these.

5 PALACIO DEL JUGO, MIAMI, FL

A selection of tropical juices at Palacio Del Jugo in Little Havana.

6 LA MAR, MIAMI, FL

A beautiful corn pudding, part of the Peruvian brunch menu at Gaston Acuria's La Mar.

7 LA CARRETA, MIAMI, FL

A Cuban sandwich at La Carreta, available all morning (and late night, too).

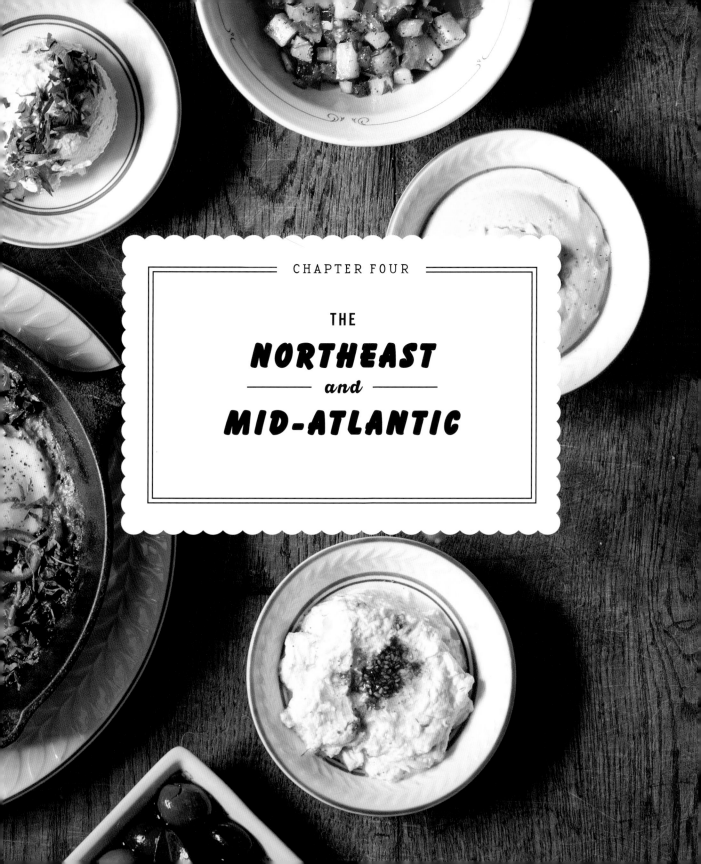

CHAPTER FOUR

THE

NORTHEAST
— and —

MID-ATLANTIC

CAMBRIDGE, MA

SOFRA
SUMMER GRANOLA 180

NEW YORK, NY

RUSS & DAUGHTERS CAFE
POTATO LATKES WITH TOPPINGS 183

BARBOUNIA
FARMER'S MARKET SHAKSHUKA 187

HOME OF CHEF GEORGETTE FARKAS OF ROTISSERIE GEORGETTE
OEUFS EN MEURETTE ON CELERY ROOT RÖSTI 190

NUM PANG NOMAD
BREAKFAST PANG WITH FENNEL-MAPLE GLAZED BACON 193

MISS LILY'S COCONUT PANCAKES 197

HOME OF DEBI MAZAR AND GABRIELE CORCOS OF THE TUSCAN GUN
FRITTATA WITH SEASONAL GREENS 198

PHILADELPHIA, PA

FEDERAL DONUTS
CAKE DONUTS 201

CAFÉ LIFT
CANNOLI FRENCH TOAST 202

HIGH STREET ON MARKET
THE FORAGER SANDWICH 205

BALTIMORE, MD

MAGGIE'S FARM
KIMCHI BRUSSELS SPROUTS, BACON, AND EGGS 208

BLUE MOON CAFE
HASH BROWNS 210

GERTRUDE'S
CRAB CAKES WITH HOMEMADE TARTAR SAUCE 211

RICHMOND, VA

MILLIE'S DINER
THE DEVIL'S MESS 212

HERITAGE
THE BIG HOT MESS 215

WASHINGTON, DC

KAPNOS
ROASTED POTATO PHYLLO PIE 218

BIRCH & BARLEY
FRIED CHICKEN AND WAFFLES 221
SCRAPPLE 224

JALEO
PUNTILLITAS SALTEADAS 225

EAST COAST SLING

It's hard to pick favorites among family, which was what choosing among the East Coast's multitude of breakfast choices felt like. In what we believe to be a contender for the greatest dining region in America—if not the world—there are limitless entry points to the first meal of the day. After much debate, we feel we've come up with a tasty cross-section of the eastern seaboard and mid-Atlantic's best dishes, acknowledging out of the gate that there is far, far more where this came from. Still, we decided to narrow the field by focusing on standouts that reflect the region's ethnic and culinary diversity. The curious invention that is scrapple prevalent all over the mid-Atlantic (see page 224); the fluffy coconut pancakes at the Jamaican joint Miss Lily's (see page 197); the poached eggs in a rich mushroom sauce that one of our favorite restaurateurs, Georgette Farkas, made for us in her charming apartment (see page 190); the potato pancakes at a storied Jewish dairy-restaurant—these were just a few of the experiences that set the day on the right course. In some cases, like the power breakfast at the legendary Loews hotel, the experience is as much about the social mores as the meal itself. Not surprising, since a New York breakfast needs to meet the needs of a busy clientele with incredibly high standards. We can't say we covered everything, but when it comes to the first meal of the day in this part of the country, we've certainly got you covered.

SUMMER GRANOLA

Makes 6 cups

As the follow-up to her award-winning Turkish-inspired restaurant, Oleana, Ana Sortun opened Sofra in partnership with her talented pastry chef, Maura Kilpatrick. Just like at Oleana, the offerings at Sofra hew to the seasons. There's always granola on the menu, but its ingredients vary based on the time of year and the whims of the chefs. This version, made extra toasty with the addition of coconut flakes and two kinds of seeds, is nice and rich thanks to a combination of coconut oil and browned butter.

Cooking spray

2¾ cups **old-fashioned rolled oats**

1½ cups **unsweetened coconut flakes**

½ cup **golden flax seeds**

1½ cups **sunflower seeds**

⅓ cup **demerara sugar,** such as Sugar in the Raw

½ teaspoon **fleur de sel** or other flaky sea salt

3 tablespoons **unsalted butter**

⅔ cup **orange blossom honey** or other mild-flavored honey

¼ cup **coconut oil**

1½ cups **dried blueberries**

1 Preheat the oven to 300°F. Line a large rimmed baking sheet with parchment paper and coat the parchment with cooking spray. Combine the oats, coconut flakes, flax seeds, sunflower seeds, sugar, and salt in a large bowl. In a medium saucepan, cook the butter over low heat until it starts to smell nutty and turn brown, 3 to 4 minutes (watch closely, as it can burn quickly). Remove the butter from the heat, add the honey and coconut oil, whisk until smooth, and pour over the oat mixture. Toss the oats with a rubber spatula to coat completely.

2 Spread the mixture in an even layer on the prepared baking sheet. Bake for 10 minutes, stir to break up the granola, then continue baking until dark golden and fragrant (the granola will get crispy once it cools), an additional 15 to 20 minutes. Cool completely, stirring occasionally to prevent the granola from sticking together. Transfer to a large bowl, add the dried blueberries, and toss. The granola will keep, stored in an airtight container, for 3 to 4 weeks.

SHARED
BLINTZES | 8
FRUIT COMPOTE, SOUR CREAM
FARMER CHEESE, RAISINS, EGG NOODLES
HALVAH ICE CREAM
HALVAH, SESAME, SALTED CAR

POTATO LATKES WITH TOPPINGS.... *Serves 6 (makes 20 to 22 latkes)*

When this century-old deli, which is a New York institution, opened a restaurant in 2014, people feared the worst: Would the spirit of the original store, serving pristine smoked, cured, and kippered fish to generations of hungry *fressers*, be lost? Thankfully, the opposite has turned out to be true. Third-generation owners Joshua Russ Tepper and Niki Russ Federman have spun off a sleek, dazzling café that's as homey as it is high-concept, fusing newfangled brunch dishes, perfectly symmetrical appetizing platters, and beet cocktails with original recipes borrowed from the deli case around the corner on Orchard Street. These potato latkes are a classic; serve them with applesauce, sour cream, chopped smoked fish, crème fraîche, even sunny-side-up eggs—pretty much everything works.

2½ pounds **Idaho or russet potatoes,** peeled
1 medium **onion**
2 large **eggs,** separated
½ cup finely chopped **scallions** (white and green parts)
¼ cup **matzo meal** or potato starch
3 tablespoons **unsalted butter,** melted
2 teaspoons **kosher salt**
½ teaspoon **freshly ground black pepper**
¼ teaspoon **baking powder**
Vegetable or canola oil, for frying

applesauce and **sour cream** or t**rout roe, flaked smoked trout,** thinly sliced **smoked salmon** and **crème fraîche**

1 Place a large fine-mesh strainer over a large bowl. Using the large holes of a box grater, grate some of the potatoes, followed by some of the onion, into the strainer, repeating until all of the potatoes and onion are grated. (Interspersing the onion prevents the potatoes from discoloring.) Using your hands, squeeze or press out as much liquid as possible, allowing the accumulated liquid to stand in the bowl for 2 to 3 minutes. Pour off the watery part, but reserve the thick, starchy paste at the bottom of the bowl (this helps bind the latkes).

2 Transfer the potato-onion mixture to a large clean bowl. Add the starchy paste, egg yolks, scallions, matzo meal, butter, salt, pepper, and baking powder and mix well. In a separate medium bowl, beat the egg whites with an electric mixer until they hold stiff, shiny peaks, 3 minutes. Fold the egg whites into the potato mixture.

recipe continues

3 In a large frying pan, heat a thin layer of oil over medium-high heat. Working in batches, scoop ¼ cup of the potato mixture into the pan for each latke. Flatten gently with a spatula and fry until the latkes are crisp and golden brown, 3 to 4 minutes per side.

4 Serve immediately with desired toppings. If the latkes cool off, reheat them in a 350°F oven for approximately 5 minutes.

An "appetizing" platter of smoked fish and all the trimmings at Russ & Daughters Café

FARMER'S MARKET SHAKSHUKA .... *Serves 4*

At the modern Mediterranean restaurant where he serves as executive chef, Amitzur Mor, who was raised in Israel, has several versions of shakshuka on his delectable brunch menu. Originally a simple skillet dish of baked eggs suspended in a rich tomato sauce, shakshuka—which means "mixture" in Tunisian and "shaken" in Hebrew—has evolved to encompass any manner of varieties and ingredients. At Barbounia the shakshuka comes in individual cast-iron vessels, but at home on his weekends off Mor constructs one giant skillet to feed a crowd. "Once you understand the basics of sautéing the vegetables, building a sauce, and finishing the eggs in the oven, the variations are endless," says Mor, who looks to his Sunday farmer's market for weekly inspiration. "The best part is, it's an entire one-pan meal in thirty to forty minutes," he adds. This green version is a mix-and-match project, allowing you to select the leafy greens and cheeses you like best.

2 tablespoons **olive oil,** plus more for drizzling

2 large **red onions,** sliced (4 cups)

1 large **leek,** white and pale green parts only, sliced and rinsed (1 cup)

3 **bell peppers,** seeded and sliced (4½ cups)

2 **jalapeño peppers,** seeded if desired and thinly sliced into discs (½ cup)

4 **garlic cloves,** minced

1 teaspoon **ground coriander**

½ teaspoon **ground cumin**

½ teaspoon **kosher salt,** or more to taste

¼ teaspoon **cayenne pepper,** or more to taste

recipe continues

1 Preheat the oven to 375°F. In a 12- or 14-inch ovenproof skillet, heat the oil over medium-low heat and cook the onions, leek, peppers, jalapeños, and garlic, stirring occasionally, until very tender, 15 to 17 minutes. Add the coriander, cumin, salt, and cayenne, stir well, and cook until incorporated, 1 to 2 minutes.

2 Working in batches, add the greens and cook, stirring, until tender, 2 to 3 minutes. Add the tomatoes and bring to a boil; reduce the heat and simmer until the liquid is reduced and the sauce is incorporated, 9 to 10 minutes. Using a spoon, form 8 wells in the sauce, gently break the eggs into them, and season with salt and pepper. Sprinkle the cheese evenly all around the eggs, then bake until the eggs are slightly firm but the yolks are still runny, 7 to 8 minutes. Garnish with the jalapeños and parsley and drizzle with some olive oil. Serve with bread.

1 pound **leafy greens,** such as baby kale, arugula, Swiss chard, or spinach, chopped

5 large ripe **tomatoes,** cored, roughly chopped, and pureed in the food processor (4 cups puree), or 4 cups **canned crushed tomatoes**

8 large **eggs**

Freshly ground black pepper to taste

½ cup shredded **kefalograviera** (see Cook's Note) or Romano cheese, or crumbled feta or goat cheese

Red or green jalapeños for garnish

2 tablespoons chopped **fresh flat-leaf parsley**

Crusty bread for serving

—————— **COOK'S NOTE** ——————

Kefalograviera is a Greek cheese typically used in the flaming appetizer known as *saganaki,* as well as for grating and seasoning. Find it at specialty Greek markets and at better cheese counters.

Power Breakfast at the Loews Regency

"My grandfather used to take me around and introduce me to all of his friends and patrons," said Jonathan Tisch as he took a seat with Lee in the dining room at the Loews Regency Hotel just above Midtown in New York City. Few people are as familiar with the property as Tisch, who serves as chairman of the Loews Hotel Group; he literally grew up on site, and his mother still lives upstairs. With his impeccably pressed bespoke suit and perfectly erect posture, he's a poster boy for the A-list clientele who frequent this room during its early-morning hours. Countless deals are sealed here over bowls of oatmeal, egg white omelets, and a steady stream of hot coffee. "You can feel the power surge in the room," said Tisch as he surveyed the tables and received visitors who popped over to say hello to him and Lee, who is also a regular power-breakfast patron at the Loews.

It was during the depths of a financial crisis in the 1970s that this New York tradition was hatched. Mayor Abe Beam joined Jonathan's father, Bob, and other movers and shakers to hatch a plan to rescue the city from its woes. The media dubbed the event "the power breakfast" and a classic Manhattan custom was born. Many businesspeople have their regular tables, and seating can be a delicate matter: individuals at opposite ends of financial transactions are often found in the same room. Still, the maître d's are expert field anthropologists, making sure everyone is comfortable—and seated to avoid prickly situations. The restaurant recently underwent a top-to-bottom makeover, and while it was closed Tisch worried that his customers might have found a new venue for breakfast. He needn't have worried. The dining room, ready to welcome a new generation of power diners, is as packed—and as powerful—as ever.

CENTER: Lee with his friend, Loews chairman Jonathan Tisch

OEUFS EN MEURETTE

ON CELERY ROOT RÖSTI ....*Serves 4*

When our friend, restaurateur Georgette Farkas of Rotisserie Georgette, heard about our breakfast project she invited us over to her home for her interpretation of Oeufs en Meurette, a dish of poached eggs in a bacon-enriched red-wine sauce that her mother made during Georgette's childhood summers in Switzerland (a version of the sauce also appears on the menu at her restaurant). This recipe makes extra sauce; use it on steaks or other grilled meats. During culinary school Farkas and her friends would often lunch on a crispy rösti—a potato pancake crisped in clarified butter—topped with a fried egg, a sort of French-speaking ploughman's lunch: inexpensive and filling. Her version replaces prosaic potatoes with the sweet surprise of celery root.

For the Sauce

6 ounces **slab bacon** or pancetta, cubed (about 1 cup)

1 medium **onion,** finely diced (about 1 cup)

1 teaspoon minced **garlic**

2 pounds **baby button mushrooms,** cleaned and quartered
 (or regular button mushrooms, diced)

2 teaspoons **fresh thyme leaves,** chopped

¼ cup **all-purpose flour**

¼ cup **tawny port**

½ cup **dry red wine**

½ cup good-quality **chicken stock**

Kosher salt and **freshly ground black pepper** to taste

recipe continues

Georgette Farkas plating her breakfast creation

1 **Make the sauce:** In a medium skillet, cook the bacon over low heat, stirring occasionally, until most of the fat is rendered, 10 minutes. With a slotted spoon, transfer the bacon to a paper towel–lined plate. Leave 2 tablespoons of the bacon fat in the skillet and discard the rest. Raise the heat to medium, add the onion, and cook, stirring, until translucent and soft, 6 to 7 minutes. Add the garlic, mushrooms, and thyme and cook, stirring, until the mushrooms are completely cooked and their liquid has evaporated, 10 minutes.

2 Add the flour and cook, stirring, for an additional 1 or 2 minutes. Add the port and wine, whisk to get rid of any lumps, and cook at a low simmer until reduced by half, 5 minutes. Return the bacon to the pan, add the chicken stock and simmer until the sauce is just thick enough to coat the back of a spoon, 3 to 4 minutes. Season with salt and pepper to taste and keep warm over a very low flame.

3 **Make the rösti:** Preheat the oven to 200°F. In a mixing bowl, combine the celery root with the parsley, eggs, flour, salt, and pepper. Heat 1 tablespoon of the clarified butter in a 6- or 7-inch crepe pan over medium heat. Add a quarter of the celery root mixture, press down to flatten, and cook, until the underside is golden brown and crisp, 8 minutes. Flip the pancake and cook until the other side is browned, 7 to 8 minutes. Transfer to a paper towel–lined baking sheet and keep warm in the oven while you fry the other rösti and poach the eggs (see page 231).

4 Warm 4 serving plates in the oven. Arrange 1 rösti on each plate, top with a poached egg, and spoon ½ cup of the sauce over each serving.

For the Rösti

2 pounds **celery root** or **parsnips**, peeled and julienned on a mandoline or shredded in a food processor
1 cup coarsely chopped **fresh flat-leaf parsley**
2 large **eggs**
¼ cup **all-purpose flour**
1 teaspoon **kosher salt**
¼ teaspoon **freshly ground black pepper**
8 tablespoons **clarified butter** (see page 212)

4 large **eggs**

--- **COOK'S NOTE** ---
For a foolproof approach that avoids the possibility of breaking the rösti while flipping, cover the pan with a plate (or even the flat removable bottom of a tart pan) and flip the pancake, crisped side up, onto the plate. Add another tablespoon of butter to the pan and slide the pancake back in to the pan, uncooked side down.

BREAKFAST PANG
WITH FENNEL-MAPLE GLAZED BACON ....*Serves 4*

At their graffiti-adorned sandwich shop just below Herald Square, partners Ben Daitz and Ratha Chaupoly—college buddies who reunited many years later in New York City—have created a sandwich sensation in the form of a pang, which we like to think of as the Cambodian banh mi. Their creations are like the hip-hop music Daitz loves: funky, unexpected, and brash, reflecting Chaupoly's Cambodian heritage and Daitz's background as a fine-dining chef. Created just for us, this sandwich contains a highly seasoned, oven-baked omelet, spice-crusted bacon, and a creamy yogurt sauce that brings it all together on a brioche bun. Luckily, you'll have leftover yogurt sauce—trust us, you'll want to put it on absolutely everything.

1 **Make the eggs:** Preheat the oven to 350°F. Lightly coat a nonstick 8-inch square baking dish or cake pan with the oil. In a large bowl whisk together the eggs, scallions, basil, sesame seeds, fish sauce, soy sauce, sriracha, and pepper. Pour the egg mixture into the baking dish and bake for 8 minutes. Rotate the pan and continue to bake the eggs until the edges are set and puffy and the center jiggles slightly when the pan is tapped, 8 to 10 minutes longer. Remove from the oven and cool for 10 minutes.

2 While the eggs bake, **make the bacon:** Set a large skillet over medium heat until hot, 1 to 2 minutes. Add the bacon (it should sizzle) and cook until crisp and golden, 7 to 8 minutes depending on thickness. Transfer the bacon to a paper towel-lined plate. Discard the fat from the skillet.

recipe continues

For the Eggs

1 tablespoon **canola oil**

8 large **eggs**

2 **scallions** (white and green parts), thinly sliced

¼ cup finely chopped **Thai basil** (or regular basil)

1 tablespoon **black sesame seeds**

1½ tablespoons **fish sauce**

1 tablespoon **soy sauce**

1 tablespoon **sriracha sauce**

½ teaspoon **freshly ground black pepper**

For the Bacon

6 slices **thick-cut bacon**

1 cup **apple cider**

2 tablespoons **maple syrup**

1½ tablespoons **apple cider vinegar**

1 tablespoon **freshly ground black pepper**

1 tablespoon **ground fennel seed**

4 **brioche buns**

½ cup **Chili Yogurt** (recipe follows)

16 **Thai basil leaves** (or regular basil leaves)

½ cup **store-bought crispy onions**, such as Onion Crunch or Lars brand

3 Pour the apple cider into the same skillet, increase the heat to medium-high, and simmer, using a wooden spoon to stir and scrape up any browned bits from the bottom of the pan, until the cider is reduced to ¼ cup, 5 to 6 minutes. Add the maple syrup, bring back to a simmer, cook for 30 seconds, then stir in the vinegar and turn off the heat. Set the glaze aside to cool slightly.

4 Toast the ground pepper and fennel in a small skillet over medium heat, shaking the pan often, until the spices become fragrant and wisps of smoke rise off the surface, 1 to 2 minutes. Transfer the spices to a large plate.

5 Slice each piece of bacon in half crosswise to yield 12 pieces, then use tongs to dip both sides of each piece of the bacon into the glaze. Dip the edges of the bacon in the spices and set aside. Invert the slightly cooled eggs onto a cutting board and cut into 4 portions equal in size to the brioche buns.

6 Slice each brioche bun in half and spread 1 tablespoon of the chili yogurt on each side. Place an egg portion over each of the bottom bun halves, then add 3 pieces of bacon. Top with 3 or 4 basil leaves and 2 tablespoons of the fried onions. Cover with the top bun half and go to town.

CHILI YOGURT ....*Makes 1¼ cups*

1 cup **plain Greek yogurt**
1½ tablespoons **sambal oelek** or sriracha
1½ teaspoons **honey**
½ teaspoon **kosher salt**
½ teaspoon **freshly ground black pepper**

Whisk all the ingredients until well combined. Store in the refrigerator in an airtight container for up to 2 weeks, stirring before use.

COCONUT PANCAKES .... *Serves 6*

Brunch at this Jamaican-themed restaurant would make a Marley proud. Riotous colors, cannabis-inspired design, and Jamaican music add up to a party every time. If you've got the brunch munchies for any reason, these tropical pancakes will hit the spot.

3 cups **sweetened shredded coconut**

4 cups **all-purpose flour**

1½ tablespoons **baking powder**

1½ teaspoons **kosher salt**

8 tablespoons (1 stick) **unsalted butter**

1½ teaspoons **honey**

3 large **eggs**

2 cups **buttermilk,** shaken

1 cup whole **milk**

2 tablespoons **coconut extract** or coconut rum

2 cups **blueberries**

½ cup **whipped butter,** room temperature (see Cook's Note)

Confectioners' sugar, for garnish

Maple syrup (optional)

1 Preheat the oven to 250°F. Spread the coconut on a large rimmed baking sheet and toast, stirring frequently, until golden brown, 20 to 25 minutes. Remove from the heat and let cool, reserving ¾ cup of the toasted coconut for garnish. Reduce the temperature to 200°F.

2 In a large bowl, whisk together the flour, baking powder, and salt. In a small skillet or a microwave, heat the butter and honey until melted; cool slightly. In a large bowl, whisk together the eggs, buttermilk, milk, and coconut extract until well incorporated, then whisk in the butter and honey. Stir the dry ingredients into the wet, mixing just until incorporated.

3 On a dry griddle or cast-iron skillet heated to medium-low, ladle the batter ½ cup at a time to form 5-inch pancakes. Cook until golden brown on the bottom and bubbly on the top, 2 to 3 minutes. Sprinkle each pancake with 2 tablespoons of the toasted coconut, flip with a spatula, and cook until golden brown on the other side, an additional 2 minutes.

4 Transfer to a plate and keep warm in the oven while continuing with the rest of the batter. Stack 3 pancakes on each plate, top with ⅓ cup of the blueberries, then dot with whipped butter and sprinkle with the reserved toasted coconut and confectioners' sugar. Serve with maple syrup.

COOK'S NOTE

Whipped butter can be bought in supermarkets or made at home by beating with a stand mixer fitted with the whisk attachment at high speed for 30 seconds.

FRITTATA WITH SEASONAL GREENS.................................*Serves 4*

At their Brooklyn home, Debi Mazar and Gabriele Corcos—stars of *Extra Virgin* on the Cooking Channel and authors of the book of the same name—are always cooking. When we arrived for breakfast on a wintry day, coffee—made Italian-style in a stovetop *macchinetta*—was ready. Gabriele laid out a spread of homemade bread and pound cake, but for us the star was this simple frittata, which Corcos—who grew up in Tuscany—has been making and eating his whole life. Unlike American-style frittatas, which can be thicker, this one is thin, with crisp, almost lacy edges. Gabriele used a box of store-bought mixed organic greens, but any tender baby greens work beautifully.

8 large **eggs**

½ cup **whole milk**

⅓ cup freshly grated **Parmigiano-Reggiano cheese**

Kosher salt and freshly ground black pepper to taste

2 tablespoons **unsalted butter**

1 5-ounce package organic seasonal **baby greens,** such as kale, chard, spinach, or a mix

1 In a large bowl, whisk the eggs, milk, and cheese and season generously with salt and pepper.

2 In a large skillet with a lid, melt the butter over medium-high heat, swirling to evenly coat. Pour the egg mixture into the pan. Using your hands, gently scatter the baby greens evenly over the eggs, pressing slightly, then cover and reduce the heat to medium-low. Cook until the edges of the frittata are almost caramelized and the vegetables are wilted, 10 minutes. Slide onto a serving platter.

FRITTATA FINESSE

AS SOMEONE WHO'S BEEN MAKING THIS DISH SINCE CHILDHOOD, Gabriele Corcos is an expert on cooking this egg dish to perfection. Since several factors can impact the dish—including the thickness of your skillet or even the tightness of the lid—checking every now and again yields the best results. "The frittata should be slightly sweaty in the center, but not stick to your fingers if you touch it," says Corcos. "Most importantly, when it's perfectly cooked, the frittata will just slide right out of the pan."

Warning: Your donuts may not look as perfect as these, but they'll taste great just the same.

CAKE DONUTS

.... *Makes 20 donuts or 40 large donut holes*

It was only fitting that Federal Donuts was the very first stop on our road trip. After all, the chef behind these irresistible sugared donuts, Michael Solomonov, is also responsible for one of the best fried chicken recipes from our last book, *Fried and True*, making him the only chef to make it into both of our projects. One taste and you'll see why.

1 **Make the batter:** In a stand mixer fitted with a paddle attachment, beat the yolks and sugar on low speed for 1 minute. Slowly add the melted butter and continue to beat on low speed until emulsified, 1 to 2 minutes. Add the buttermilk and mix for 30 seconds.

2 In a separate bowl, whisk the flour, salt, baking soda, baking powder, and pumpkin pie spice. Add the dry ingredients to the mixer and beat on low speed for 2 minutes. Raise the speed to medium and beat for an additional minute until the batter is smooth and homogenous.

3 **Fry the donuts:** Set a wire rack over a baking sheet and set aside. Fill a 4-quart stockpot with 8 cups vegetable shortening or oil. Using a candy thermometer, heat the oil to 375°F. Use a donut batter or pancake dispenser to drop batter into the pot (if it's easier, use a 2-tablespoon cookie scoop and just make donut holes). Fry until golden brown, 1 to 2 minutes per side, allowing oil to come up to temperature between batches. Cool slightly on a rack.

4 **Sugar the donuts:** Combine the sugar and spice in a bowl. While hot, roll each donut in the seasoned sugar.

For the Donuts

10 **egg yolks**

2 cups **sugar**

5 tablespoons **butter,** melted and slightly cooled

1¼ cups **buttermilk**

4½ cups **flour**

2 teaspoons **fine sea salt**

1 teaspoon **baking powder**

1 teaspoon **baking soda**

2 teaspoons **pumpkin pie spice** or Baharat spice (See Cook's Note)

Vegetable shortening or vegetable oil, for frying

For the Seasoned Sugar

1 cup **sugar**

2 teaspoons **pumpkin pie spice** or Baharat spice

─────── **COOK'S NOTE** ───────

Baharat is a spice blend made especially for Solomonov by Lior Lev Sercarz at La Boîte in New York; it can be ordered online at www.laboiteny.com

CANNOLI FRENCH TOAST ....*Serves 4*

Café Lift chef and owner Michael Pasquarello created this French toast as a nod to the South Philly of his youth. "It was Calabria number two," said Pasquarello of the neighborhood where he grew up, and where his grandmother made her own cannoli—right down to the shells. He's taken the best elements of the classic Italian treat—sweetened ricotta, toasty pistachios, a bit of chocolate—and turned them into a decadent morning indulgence that also works as an after-dinner dessert.

For the Cannoli Filling

2 cups good-quality **ricotta cheese**

½ cup **confectioners' sugar,** plus more for dusting

½ teaspoon **vanilla extract**

½ teaspoon grated **lemon zest**

For the French Toast

5 large **eggs**

½ cup **half-and-half**

3 tablespoons **sugar**

1 tablespoon **cinnamon**

½ teaspoon **vanilla extract**

8 tablespoons (1 stick) **unsalted butter**

¼ cup **vegetable oil**

1 large loaf of day-old **challah** or brioche, cut into 2-inch-thick slices

½ cup chopped **pistachios**, toasted

½ cup chopped **bittersweet chocolate**

2 **bananas**, sliced

recipe continues

1 **Make the filling:** Line a medium strainer with cheesecloth and set over a bowl. Place the ricotta in the strainer and let drain in the refrigerator overnight; discard the liquid. In a large bowl, vigorously whisk the ricotta with the confectioners' sugar, vanilla, and lemon zest.

2 **Make the French toast:** Preheat the oven to 350°F. In a large bowl, whisk the eggs, half-and-half, sugar, cinnamon, and vanilla. In a large skillet, heat 2 tablespoons of the butter and 1 tablespoon of the vegetable oil over high heat until the butter just turns golden. Reduce the heat to medium. Dip 2 pieces of the challah in the batter for 10 seconds, shake off the excess, and place in the pan. Cook until golden, shaking the pan after 1 minute to loosen the bread, 2 to 3 minutes total. Flip and cook until the second side is golden, 2 to 3 minutes more.

3 Transfer to a baking sheet, then repeat with the remaining butter, oil, bread, and batter. Place the baking sheet in the oven and bake the French toast until deep golden, 10 minutes.

4 Divide the French toast among 4 plates and top with ½ cup of the filling. Garnish each plate with the pistachios, chocolate, and bananas and dust with additional confectioners' sugar.

THE FORAGER SANDWICH .... *Serves 4*

Every morning this Philadelphia standout begins with a prodigious offering of house-baked breads, pastries, and sandwiches. And in a town where breakfast sandwiches are a way of life, this elevated example is a paragon of Philly's best. Here, chef Eli Kulp has created an offering designed to please vegetarians and carnivores alike. Kulp starts out with a mushroom-infused mayo that improves everything it touches, and the marinated royal trumpet mushrooms—also known as king oysters—are every bit as meaty as steak, making this a worthy breakfast-for-dinner option.

1 ***Marinate the mushrooms:*** In a medium skillet or small saucepan, heat the oil over medium-low heat. Add the shallot and garlic and cook, stirring, until softened, 2 to 3 minutes. Add the wine, vinegar, thyme, and bay leaf and bring to a boil. Simmer until reduced by half, 7 to 8 minutes. Place the royal trumpet mushrooms in a heatproof container, pour over the hot mixture, and cool to room temperature, 30 minutes. Cover tightly and refrigerate overnight.

2 ***Cook the kale:*** In a large skillet, heat the oil over medium heat. Add the onion and cook, stirring, until softened, 3 minutes. Add the garlic and cook for 1 additional minute. Add the kale in two batches and cook, stirring, until wilted, 3 minutes total. Add the pepper flakes, remove from the heat, and cool slightly.

recipe continues

For the Marinated Mushrooms

¼ cup **olive oil**

½ **shallot,** thinly sliced

1 **garlic clove,** thinly sliced

1 cup **dry white wine**

½ cup **white wine vinegar**

1 sprig of **fresh thyme**

1 **bay leaf**

4 large **royal trumpet mushrooms,** tough ends trimmed, sliced lengthwise ⅛ inch thick, and lightly scored on both sides (see Cook's Note)

For the Kale

2 tablespoons **olive oil**

1 **onion,** finely chopped

4 **garlic cloves,** minced

8 large **kale leaves,** stems removed, trimmed and chopped

½ teaspoon **dried red pepper flakes**

3 *Make the mushroom mayo:* Place the dried mushrooms in a small bowl, cover with boiling water, and soak until softened, 10 minutes. Drain, squeezing out the excess liquid, then roughly chop. In a medium skillet heat the oil over medium-high heat. Add the rehydrated mushrooms, chopped creminis, garlic, and shallot and cook, stirring, until the mushrooms release their water, 5 minutes. Add the rosemary, salt, pepper, and sherry vinegar, stir well, remove from heat, and let cool. In the small bowl of a food processor, pulse the mushroom mixture until finely chopped. Add the mayonnaise, blend until smooth, and season with additional salt and pepper to taste. Mayonnaise keeps chilled in an airtight container for 3 to 4 days.

4 *Cook the mushrooms:* Remove the thyme and bay leaf and drain and discard the liquid. Heat a griddle or grill pan over medium-high heat and sear the mushrooms until charred, 2 minutes per side.

5 *Assemble the sandwiches:* Preheat the broiler. Cook the eggs sunny-side up (see page 233). Spread both sides of each roll with 1 tablespoon of the mayo. Arrange some mushroom slices on the bottom half of each roll followed by 1 cup of the kale, 1 egg, and 1 slice of cheese. Place under the broiler until the cheese is melted, 1 minute. Cover with the Kaiser roll tops.

For the Mushroom Mayo

¼ cup **dried black trumpet mushrooms**
1 tablespoon **olive oil**
½ cup chopped **cremini mushrooms**
1 **garlic clove,** minced
½ medium **shallot,** minced
2 teaspoons chopped **fresh rosemary**
¼ teaspoon **kosher salt,** plus more to taste
¼ teaspoon **freshly ground black pepper,** plus more to taste
1 tablespoon **sherry vinegar**
1 cup **mayonnaise,** such as Hellman's

For the sandwiches

4 large **eggs**
Oil and/or butter for frying the eggs
4 **Kaiser rolls,** split, lightly toasted, and lightly buttered
4 slices **Swiss cheese**

--- **COOK'S NOTE** ---

Trumpet mushrooms, also known as king oyster mushrooms, are meaty mushrooms that don't need to be trimmed as aggressively as many other varieties; in this case, the stem provides as much flavor as the cap. If you can't find king oysters, use large oyster mushrooms—they'll stand in nicely.

KIMCHI BRUSSELS SPROUTS, BACON, AND EGGS ....*Serves 6*

With its rustic name and reputation for seasonal, farm-fresh cuisine, this four-year-old Charm City favorite might be expected to exude a prairie vibe. That's why we were surprised to find a dining room with pressed-tin ceilings, dark-wood accents, and a tattooed staff that suggested "speakeasy" as much as anything else (even cooler is the restaurant's name, which is inspired by an obscure 1965 Bob Dylan song). We loved these crispy, salty, meaty Brussels sprouts on the weekend brunch menu, which do double duty as either a hearty side dish or, when topped with sunny-side-up eggs, a standalone morning main course. At the restaurant they use a house-made kimchi, but chef Tim Hogan went easy on us, allowing a store-bought substitute that doesn't compromise this dish's unique characteristics.

Vegetable oil, for frying

1¼ pounds **Brussels sprouts**

¾ cup packed **kimchi**

4 ounces diced **pancetta** or thick-cut bacon (about ½ cup)

1½ teaspoons **kosher salt**

1 teaspoon **freshly ground black pepper**

6 large **eggs,** at room temperature

1 Fill a large, tall pot with 4 inches of oil and heat the oil to 365°F, making sure to use a pot that has at least 10 inches of space over the oil. Meanwhile, trim the ends from the Brussels sprouts, discard the outer leaves, and halve the sprouts (or quarter them if they're large). Working in 2 batches, gently lower the sprouts into the hot oil and fry until crispy, 3 to 4 minutes (the oil will drop to about 340 to 345°F, so make sure to bring the oil back up to temperature between batches). Drain on paper towels and season with the salt and pepper.

2 Using your hands, squeeze all of the excess liquid from the kimchi into a small bowl and reserve the liquid. Roughly chop the kimchi and set aside.

3 In a 10- or 12-inch skillet, cook the pancetta over medium-high heat until crispy, 5 to 6 minutes. Remove the pancetta with a slotted spoon to a paper towel–lined plate; drain and discard the fat.

4 Add the kimchi liquid to the same skillet and cook, stirring, until warmed through, 2 to 3 minutes. Add the sprouts, pancetta, and chopped kimchi and cook, stirring, until hot, 2 to 3 minutes.

5 Cook the eggs, sunny-side up (see page 233). Divide the sprout mixture evenly among 4 bowls and top each bowl with a cooked egg.

HASH BROWNS .... *Serves 2*

We sought out Baltimore's Blue Moon Cafe for their over-the-top, almost architectural take on French toast. But then plates began passing by and catching our attention: cheesy omelets filled with the most alluring hash browns we'd ever seen, golden and lacy with the promise of great crunch. We quickly added them to our order, and those browns lived up to every expectation. The secret to making them is counterintuitive: as opposed to preheating oil on a griddle, you mound freshly shredded potatoes directly onto a piping-hot, un-oiled surface, then stream a butter-oil mixture on top. The alchemy of iron, oil, and spuds added up to the texture of our dreams.

3 tablespoons **vegetable oil**

2 tablespoons **melted butter**

3/4 teaspoon **kosher salt**

1 large **Russet potato,** peeled

1/2 teaspoon **freshly ground black pepper**

1 Combine the oil, butter, and 1/2 teaspoon of the salt in a bowl and whisk to dissolve the salt.

2 Heat a cast-iron skillet over medium-high heat (do not oil the pan). While the pan is heating, grate the potato into a bowl and toss it with the remaining 1/4 teaspoon salt and the pepper. Add the potato mixture to the skillet and spread it out into a loose circle about 1/2-inch thick.

3 Drizzle half the butter mixture evenly over the potatoes and cook without moving until the bottom is golden, 4 to 5 minutes. Flip the potatoes, then add the rest of the butter mixture on top of the potatoes and cook until the bottom is golden and crunchy, 4 to 5 minutes. Transfer to a paper towel–lined plate and serve hot.

CRAB CAKES

WITH HOMEMADE TARTAR SAUCE AND SUNNY-SIDE-UP EGGS .... *Serves 4*

Baltimore is a crab-cake town, and there are almost as many variations as there are restaurateurs. But for the gold standard we turned to John Shields, whose whole restaurant is inspired by his grandma Gertie, and the crab cake that started it all for this award-winning chef. The secret is to bind the cakes until they just hold together in their uncooked state; they may seem as if they'll fall apart, but a good fry brings them together to crispy perfection.

1 ***Make the tartar sauce:*** In a bowl, combine all of the ingredients and refrigerate for at least 1 hour to let the flavors meld.

2 ***Make the crab cakes:*** Line a baking sheet with waxed paper and set aside. In a bowl whisk together the egg, mayonnaise, mustard, pepper, Old Bay, Worcestershire, and Tabasco together until frothy. In a separate bowl add the crabmeat and sprinkle the cracker crumbs on top. Pour the egg mixture on top and gently toss or fold, taking care not to break up the lumps of crab.

3 Using an ice cream scoop, divide the crabmeat into 8 mounds about 3 inches in diameter and ¾ inch thick (the cakes should feel loose but they should still hold their shape). Arrange the crab cakes on the prepared baking sheet, cover, and refrigerate for at least 1 hour.

4 In a large, heavy skillet heat 1½ inches oil over medium heat. Working in batches, fry the crab cakes until golden brown, 4 minutes per side. Drain on paper towels. Cook the eggs sunny-side up (see page 233). Serve with the tartar sauce and the eggs.

For the tartar sauce (makes 1½ cups):

1 cup **mayonnaise**
½ cup finely chopped **dill pickle**
¼ cup minced **onion**
2 tablespoons chopped **fresh flat-leaf parsley**
1 tablespoon **dill pickle juice**

For the crab cakes:

1 **egg**
2 heaping tablespoons **mayonnaise**
1 teaspoon **dry mustard**
½ teaspoon **freshly ground black pepper**
1 teaspoon **Old Bay seasoning**
2 teaspoons **Worcestershire sauce**
Dash of **Tabasco Sauce**
1 pound **lump crabmeat**, picked over
¼ cup crushed **Saltine crackers**
Vegetable oil, for frying
Clarified butter and olive oil, for sautéing

—————— **COOK'S NOTE** ——————
If you have any accompanying tartar sauce left over, serve it with fish sandwiches, or stir into tuna salad.

THE DEVIL'S MESS .... *Serves 6*

In 1775 Patrick Henry delivered his famous speech from the steps of Richmond's St. John's Church: "Give me liberty, or give me death!" These days, the city's residents often do their begging at the doorstep of Millie's Diner, where a weekend table for brunch is as hard to come by as a blast of cool air in July. "We have a wild party here every Sunday," said co-owner Paul Keevil as he welcomed us inside the eclectically decorated restaurant on a scorching summer day. A six-burner stove wedged in the front serves as the locus of operations for cooks in constant motion, slinging ingredients onto the sizzling flattop for plate after plate of delicious dishes. One of the most-requested dishes is the Devil's Mess, a spicy scramble of eggs, peppers, sausage, and cheese that Paul—a former rock 'n' roller and British expat—sees as a modern homage to the beloved "full English" breakfast of his childhood.

1 Preheat the broiler. In a 12- or 14-inch ovenproof nonstick skillet, cook the sausage over medium-high heat, breaking up the meat with a wooden spoon or a spatula, until browned, 6 to 7 minutes. Transfer the sausage to a bowl, drain off the excess liquid, and set aside.

2 In the same skillet heat the butter over medium heat. Add the onion and pepper and cook, stirring, until the onion is translucent, 5 to 6 minutes. Add the garlic and spices and cook, stirring, for 30 seconds. Return the sausage to the skillet along with the tomatoes and wine and bring to a boil; then reduce the heat to medium-low and cook until the liquid has evaporated, 2 to 3 minutes.

recipe continues

1 pound **spicy Italian sausage** (about 5 links), casings removed

2 tablespoons **clarified or melted butter** (see Tip)

1 medium **onion,** chopped (1 cup)

1 medium **green pepper,** chopped (1 cup)

2 **garlic cloves,** minced

1 teaspoon **ground cumin**

½ teaspoon **ground ginger** (see Cook's Note)

½ teaspoon **ground cardamom**

½ teaspoon **ground fenugreek**

½ teaspoon **ground turmeric**

½ teaspoon **cayenne pepper,** or to taste

1 cup chopped fresh **tomatoes** (or 1 cup canned diced tomatoes)

¼ cup **dry red wine**

6 large **eggs,** lightly beaten

2 cups grated **sharp Cheddar cheese**

1 **avocado,** sliced

——— COOK'S NOTE ———

One tablespoon curry powder can be substituted for the ginger, cardamom, fenugreek, turmeric, and cayenne.

3 Add the eggs and stir until nearly set, 2 minutes. Top with the cheese, transfer to the broiler, and broil until the cheese is melted and the eggs are firm, rotating the pan if necessary, 2 to 3 minutes. Garnish with the avocado.

CLARIFIED BUTTER

WHAT'S BETTER THAN BUTTER? Not much. But using it for frying can be tricky, since the milk solids and protein tend to burn. To sidestep this problem, clarify butter by bringing a stick or two to a low simmer in a small (1- or 2-quart) saucepan for 3 to 4 minutes. Skim the white foam off the top, then gently tip the butter into a tight-sealing jar, leaving the white residue at the bottom of the saucepan. Clarified butter will keep, tightly sealed, in the fridge for up to 2 months.

THE BIG HOT MESS ....*Serves 6 to 8*

It's no secret that chefs like to unwind with a night of drinking after a long shift on the line—and pay the price the next morning, when showing up at work is non-negotiable. At his award-winning restaurant, Chef Joe Sparatta offers this richer-than-rich dish on his brunch menu, but many of its biggest fans remain in the back of the house, where Sparatta slings this hash with enthusiasm to cure what ails his staff. Slow-braised short ribs, a rich sauce, crispy potatoes, and a creamy aïoli add up to the ultimate hangover cure.

1 **Cook the short ribs:** Preheat the oven to 350°F. Heat a Dutch oven over high heat. Season the short ribs with salt and pepper and sear the short ribs until browned, 2 to 3 minutes per side. Transfer to a plate and set aside, leaving the rendered fat in the pot. Lower the heat to medium, add the onion, carrot, celery, and garlic and sauté until the vegetables begin to soften, stirring occasionally, 6 to 7 minutes.

2 Return the short ribs and any accumulated juices back to the pot with the bay leaf, add the chicken stock, cover, and braise in the oven until the meat is almost tender, 2 hours. Cool for at least 1 hour and up to 4 hours. Remove the meat from the sauce, and shred the meat for the mess, discarding the fat and bones. Skim the liquid and reserve for another use.

3 Meanwhile, **make the tomato aïoli:** Heat the oil in a medium skillet on medium-low heat. Add the onion and garlic and cook, stirring, until softened, 5 minutes. Add the tomato sauce and continue to cook, stirring occasionally, until it reduces to a paste consistency, 5 to 6 minutes. Remove from the heat, cool slightly, and transfer to the small

For the Short Ribs

3 pounds **bone-in short ribs**

Kosher salt and **freshly ground black pepper**

1 large **onion,** diced (2 cups)

1 large **carrot,** diced (¾ cup)

3 **celery stalks,** diced (1 cup)

4 **garlic cloves,** thinly sliced

1 **bay leaf**

6 cups **chicken stock**

For the Tomato Aïoli

1 tablespoon **canola oil**

½ medium **onion,** diced

10 **garlic cloves,** sliced

1 8-ounce can **tomato sauce**

1 teaspoon **sriracha sauce**

⅛ teaspoon **liquid smoke**

⅓ cup **mayonnaise**

bowl of a food processor. Add the sriracha and liquid smoke and process until smooth, scraping down the sides of the bowl if necessary, 30 seconds. Add the mayonnaise and process until incorporated and smooth, 15 seconds. Transfer to a bowl, cover, and refrigerate until ready to use.

4 ***Prepare the cream cheese:*** Heat the oven to 450°F. Place the jalapeño on a double layer of foil and roast until soft, 30 minutes. Cool slightly, discard the skin and seeds, and place the flesh in the small bowl of a food processor along with the cream cheese and salt. Process until smooth and well incorporated, scraping down the sides of the bowl once or twice, 30 seconds total. Transfer to a large Ziploc bag (you will use this to pipe the cream cheese), seal, and refrigerate until ready to use.

5 ***Cook the potatoes:*** Place the potatoes in a large pot, cover with 2 inches of cold water, bring to a boil, and simmer until they become soft, 20 minutes. While the potatoes are cooking, preheat the oil in a large pot to 350°F. Drain the potatoes, let them dry for 2 minutes, then, while they are still hot, cut them into large cubes. Working in batches, fry the potatoes until golden brown, 6 to 7 minutes. Drain on a paper towel–lined plate and season with salt and pepper to taste. Repeat with the remaining potatoes, giving the oil time to return to temperature between batches.

6 ***Make the mess:*** Preheat the broiler. In a baking pan, layer the fried potatoes and the shredded short rib meat. Snip the corner of the Ziploc bag containing the cream cheese and pipe the cream cheese all over the rib meat. Cover the pan with the shredded cheese. Place under the broiler until browned, bubbly, and warmed through, 2 to 4 minutes. Meanwhile, cook the eggs in any style you wish (see pages 231–233), if desired. Top the mess with the aïoli, garnish with chives, and serve with the eggs.

For the Cream Cheese

1 small **jalapeño pepper**

1 8-ounce package **cream cheese**

1 teaspoon **smoked salt** (or
    1 teaspoon salt mixed with
    ½ teaspoon smoked paprika)

For the Potatoes

6 medium **Idaho or Russet potatoes**
    (3 pounds), scrubbed, peels on

Canola oil, for deep frying

Kosher salt and **freshly ground black
    pepper** to taste

For the Hot Mess

2½ cups (10 ounces) shredded **sharp
    Cheddar cheese**

6 **eggs** (optional)

¼ cup chopped **chives,** for garnish

ROASTED POTATO PHYLLO PIE ....*Serves 8*

Raised in a tight-knit family in Alexandria, Virginia, Kapnos co-owner and executive chef George Pagonis practically grew up in his family's Greek diner. Though he never left his roots behind, he logged time in fine-dining kitchens in New York and DC before partnering with chef Mike Isabella to open Kapnos, a modern taverna heavily informed by Pagonis's Proustian yearnings. In this flaky phyllo crescent, Pagonis fills the crispy, papery layers with yogurt-cloaked potatoes, then places the pie atop a decadent, smoky romesco sauce and tops it with an herb salad studded with crunchy nuts.

1 **Make the Romesco:** Preheat the broiler to high. Arrange the peppers on a foil-lined baking sheet and broil on all sides, turning every few minutes, until the skins become charred and the flesh is soft, 20 to 25 minutes. Place the peppers in a heatproof bowl and cover with plastic wrap until cool enough to handle. Reduce the oven temperature to 375°F. Peel the peppers, discarding the skins and seeds.

2 In a blender, puree the peppers, ½ cup of the almonds, 2 tablespoons of the olive oil, the vinegar, and ½ teaspoon of the salt until smooth, 1 minute. Transfer to a bowl and whisk in the 2 tablespoons yogurt.

3 **Prepare the pies:** Toss the potatoes with 2 tablespoons of the oil and ½ teaspoon of the salt. Place on a baking sheet and bake at 375°F until cooked through, 25 minutes. Let cool, then slice into ¼-inch-thick discs. In a medium bowl, toss the potatoes with the 2 cups yogurt, the scallions, roasted garlic, and ½ teaspoon of the salt. Cover and chill for 30 minutes.

recipe continues

For the Romesco

3 large **red bell peppers**

1 cup chopped **almonds**, lightly toasted

5 tablespoons **extra-virgin olive oil**, divided

1 tablespoon **red wine vinegar**

2 teaspoons **kosher salt**, divided

2 cups plus 2 tablespoons **plain whole-milk Greek yogurt**

For the pies

1 pound **fingerling potatoes**

6 large **scallions** (white and green parts), thinly sliced (¾ cup)

1 tablespoon **roasted garlic**, pureed (see Cook's Note)

8 tablespoons (1 stick) **unsalted butter**, melted

16 standard sheets **phyllo dough**, thawed

8 large **eggs**

For the salad

⅔ cup packed **fresh flat-leaf parsley leaves**

⅔ cup packed **fresh dill**

⅔ cup snipped **fresh chives**, cut into 1-inch pieces

1½ teaspoons lemon juice

4 Raise the heat to 425°F and brush a large baking sheet with melted butter. On a large, clean work surface, unroll the phyllo sheets, keeping them well covered with a kitchen towel. Place one sheet of phyllo on the work surface and brush with melted butter. Set another sheet on top and brush with additional butter.

5 Arrange ½ cup of the potato mixture lengthwise in a line across the phyllo, at least 2 inches from the bottom and 1 inch from the sides. Roll the phyllo over the mixture very gently but tightly, to prevent air pockets; pinch the edges shut. When you finish rolling you will have one large cigar-like cylinder. Brush lightly with melted butter and very carefully coil into a spiral. Place the pie on the prepared baking sheet and repeat with the remaining 7 pies. Bake until golden and flaky, turning once midway, 25 minutes.

6 *Make the salad:* In a bowl toss the parsley, dill, chives, and remaining ½ cup chopped almonds with the remaining 1 tablespoon olive oil, the lemon juice, and ½ teaspoon salt, or to taste. Prepare the eggs, sunny-side up (see page 233). To serve, spoon ¼ cup romesco sauce onto a plate, top with a phyllo pie and an egg, and garnish with ¼ cup of the herb salad.

COOK'S NOTE

To roast garlic, preheat the oven to 375°F. Cut ¼ inch from the top of a head of garlic. Place in a square of aluminum foil, drizzle with 1 tablespoon olive oil, sprinkle with salt and pepper, seal, and roast until the cloves are soft, 30 to 35 minutes. Let cool.

FRIED CHICKEN & WAFFLES .... *Serves 8*

No one's quite sure where the tradition of pairing fried chicken and crispy waffles first originated (some believe it was at Roscoe's in Los Angeles). At any rate, we found a new favorite in our nation's capital, where many turn to Birch & Barley for a gold-standard representation of a now-iconic American dish. Chef Kyle Bailey shared his sumptuous version, one of the stars of a brunch menu that draws crowds—and long lines—every weekend. He wisely selects chicken thighs to brine in buttermilk and spices before dredging them in a heavily seasoned flour mixture and frying to a shattering crispness; the thighs never lose their natural juiciness.

1 *Marinate the chicken:* Combine the buttermilk, onion powder, pepper, salt, and cayenne in a large glass mixing bowl or ziptop bag. Add the chicken and submerge to coat completely. Cover and refrigerate for 12 hours and up to overnight.

2 *Make the waffles:* Preheat the oven to 250°F. In a medium saucepan, warm ¼ cup of milk with the ¼ teaspoon sugar over low heat for 2 minutes. Remove from the heat, add the yeast, and let it bloom until it foams, 15 minutes.

3 Add the remaining sugar, the melted butter, and egg yolks to the milk-yeast mixture and whisk to combine. Whisk in the flour, alternating with the remaining 2½ cups of milk, until smooth. In a stand mixer fitted with the whisk attachment, whip the egg whites until they form stiff peaks, 3 minutes on high speed, then fold them into the waffle batter.

recipe continues

For the Marinade

2 cups **buttermilk**

2 teaspoons **onion powder**

1 teaspoon **freshly ground black pepper**

1 teaspoon **kosher salt**

½ teaspoon **cayenne pepper**

8 **boneless, skinless chicken thighs**

For the Waffles

2¾ cups **milk**, divided

⅓ cup plus ¼ teaspoon **sugar**, divided

¼ teaspoon **active dry yeast**

7 tablespoons **unsalted butter, melted,** plus more for greasing the waffle iron

2 large **eggs**, separated

3¼ cups **all-purpose flour**

For the Coating

Canola oil, for frying

1½ cups **all-purpose flour**

1 teaspoon **onion powder**

½ teaspoon **freshly ground black pepper**

½ teaspoon **kosher salt**

¼ teaspoon **cayenne pepper**

1 cup **buttermilk**

Cooked, crispy bacon and **maple syrup,** for serving

4 Grease a waffle iron with butter and cook the waffles, 1/2 cup batter at a time, according to the manufacturer's instructions. Keep the waffles warm on a sheet pan in the oven while you fry the chicken.

5 ***Fry the chicken:*** Fill a cast-iron skillet with 1 1/2 inches of oil and heat to 350°F.

6 In a medium mixing bowl, whisk the flour, onion powder, pepper, salt, and cayenne. Place the buttermilk in a separate bowl. Remove the chicken from the marinade, letting the excess drip off. Coat the chicken in the flour mixture first, then the buttermilk, then the flour mixture again, shaking off the excess at each step.

7 Working in batches, fry the chicken until golden brown and cooked through (until a thermometer reaches 165°F when inserted into the thickest part), turning once, 7 to 8 minutes, letting oil return to temperature between batches. Transfer to a plate and keep warm in the oven between batches. Serve immediately with bacon and maple syrup.

SCRAPPLE

Serves 6

If you've ever been to a diner in the mid-Atlantic, there's a good chance you'll see scrapple on the menu. Typically a blend of meat scraps, offal, and pork fat bound together with starchy cornmeal or oats, scrapple is thought to have arrived in the United States with German immigrants in the 1700s. Fried to a crisp after being chilled and cut into slices, it's a sort of country terrine for regular folk. Here, chef Kyle Bailey replaces the offal with easier-to-find chicken livers.

6 ounces **pork butt**, diced
4 ounces **raw chicken livers** (about 3)
1½ cups **chicken stock**
½ teaspoon **salt**
½ teaspoon **freshly ground black pepper**
Pinch of **dried red pepper flakes**
Pinch of **freshly chopped sage**
Pinch of **mace**
Pinch of **nutmeg**
⅓ cup **cornmeal**
2 tablespoons **rolled oats**

1 In a medium saucepan, combine the pork butt, livers, and chicken stock, bring to a boil, then lower the heat and simmer until the pork is tender, 10 minutes. Remove the pork and chicken livers. Using the large die attachment on a stand mixer, grind the pork and livers, or use a food processor and pulse the meat until fine (about 10 to 15 pulses).

2 Return the mixture to the saucepan, stir the salt, pepper, red pepper flakes, sage, mace, and nutmeg and bring the mixture to a simmer over medium heat. Whisk in the cornmeal and rolled oats, reduce the heat to low, and cook, stirring constantly, until the mixture achieves a porridge-like texture, 10 minutes. Cool for 10 minutes.

3 Line a mini (8-ounce) loaf pan with plastic wrap, leaving 4 inches of overhang on each side. Pour the mixture into the pan, then cover with the plastic wrap and refrigerate overnight.

4 Heat 1 tablespoon oil in a skillet over medium heat. Slice the scrapple into ¼-inch slices and pan-sear on both sides until golden brown, 1 to 2 minutes per side.

PUNTILLITAS SALTEADAS ....*Serves 4*

When Spanish chef José Andrès visits Barcelona, one of his first stops is Bar Pinotxo, a counter-only restaurant inside Barcelona's storied Boqueria market that opens early. Though it's known for a host of incredible dishes, seafood preparations are a highlight. Come breakfast time you'll find early-morning diners feasting on baby squid from the Cádiz region, flash cooked with white beans, olive oil, and garlic (a glass of cava, while optional, is highly recommended). Andrès re-created the dish just for us. Though he imports baby squid from Spain to make the dish at his restaurant, Jaleo, we found more readily available standard calamari a very suitable swap-in.

In a large skillet heat ¼ cup of the oil over medium-high heat. Add the squid and cook, stirring, until just cooked through and the edges begin to turn golden, 2 minutes. Add the garlic and cook, stirring, until fragrant, 30 seconds. Add the beans, 2 more tablespoons of the oil, and the salt and cook, stirring, until warmed through, an additional 30 seconds to 1 minute. Divide among 4 plates, drizzle with the remaining olive oil, and garnish with parsley.

½ cup **extra-virgin olive oil,** preferably Spanish, divided

1 pound **fresh squid** body, cleaned and sliced into thin rings

¼ cup minced **garlic**

3 15-ounce cans **small white beans** (such as alubias, navy, or cannellini), drained and rinsed

1 teaspoon **salt**

4 teaspoons chopped **fresh flat-leaf parsley,** for garnish

MORE NORTHEAST CLASSICS

1 BALTHAZAR, NEW YORK, NY

A vol au vent at Balthazar, a downtown Manhattan breakfast and brunch classic since 1997.

2 MORIMOTO, PHILADELPHIA, PA

A re-creation of a classic "Fancy Japanese hotel breakfast," beloved by Chef Masaharu Morimoto. He re-created his favorite dishes just for us, including a dish of spicy mullet roe wrapped in sweetened seaweed sheets.

3 GERTRUDE'S, BALTIMORE, MD

Chef John Shield's crabcakes are a classic menu item (see page 211).

4 A CORNER DELI SPECIAL, NEW YORK, NY

Cheap, filling, and delicious, a BEC (bacon, egg, and cheese) on a roll fuels the morning for tens of thousands of New Yorkers thanks to its ubiquity at countless corner markets. Here, a classic version at an uptown bodega.

5 TED'S BULLETIN, WASHINGTON, D.C.

Hundreds of these breakfast pastries in a multitude of flavors are sold daily.

6 EGG, BROOKLYN, NY

George Weld at Egg, his Williamsburg, Brooklyn, restaurant, which was one of the first in New York to serve an exclusively breakfast-focused menu.

SUNDAY, BLOODY SUNDAY

No matter where we traveled, one item turned up in virtually every weekend menu: the Bloody Mary. Perhaps because it's the perfect hair-of-the-dog beverage, or because it eats like a meal when you may not quite yet be ready for truly solid repast— the Bloody Mary always comes through. Every time we rolled into a new city, we eagerly scanned restaurant menus for the most inventive takes on this cocktail classic. Here are some of our favorites.

1 27, MIAMI

With a green tomato and a cucumber ribbon

2 BACHELOR FARMER, MINNEAPOLIS

A Red Snapper, made with Sochu and Malbec,

3 THE BEVERLY HILTON, BEVERLY HILLS

Garnished with bacon and stuffed olives

4 BLD, LOS ANGELES

A Michelada Bloody Mary

5 COMMANDERS PALACE, NEW ORLEANS

Embellished with pickled okra and peppadew peppers

6 DUCKS EATERY, NEW YORK CITY

Decked out with smoked mussels, bacon, and charred lemons

7 GERTRUDE'S, BALTIMORE

A shrimp cocktail bloody

8 JALEO, WASHINGTON, DC

With baby clams

9 KAPNOS, WASHINGTON, DC

Topped with a grilled green tomato and serrano chile

10 GENNESSEE ROYAL, KANSAS CITY

This creative crab claw-topped bloody grabbed our attention immediately.

11 PERENNIAL VIRANT, CHICAGO

Made savory with a house-made "slim jim," cheese, and pickled asparagus

12 ROOSTER, ST. LOUIS

Spiced with wasabi peas

13 SUNSHINE TAVERN, PORTLAND

Salami and a beer chaser on the side,

14 TASTY N SONS, PORTLAND

Packed with pickled beets and mushrooms

15 THE BRISTOL, CHICAGO

Smoky with charred pickled vegetables

HOW TO GET PERFECT EGGS EVERY TIME

Eggs are at the heart of many of the recipes in this book, and knowing how to cook them properly can make the difference between good and great dishes. Follow these easy instructions for no-fail eggs every time.

Soft-Scrambled

Gently whisk 3 eggs with 2 tablespoons heavy cream in a bowl. Heat 1 tablespoon unsalted butter in a nonstick skillet over low heat. Add the eggs and cook, stirring constantly, until they start becoming custard-like. Be patient; your instinct will be to raise the temperature or to stop stirring, but this will compromise the softness of the eggs. When the eggs are still wet but appear creamy and cohesive, add chopped fresh herbs and season with salt.

Poached

Bring a saucepan filled with 4 inches of water to a boil. Crack 1 egg into a small glass bowl. Add ½ teaspoon white vinegar to the water. Using a large spoon, swirl the water near the rim of the pan to create a centrifuge. While the water is still moving, get the bowl as close to the surface as you can and slip the egg into the water. Reduce the heat to a bubbling simmer and cook the egg, not moving it, until the white is opaque, 2 to 3 minutes. You may see strands of white floating on the body of the egg; don't worry, they'll either float off or meld themselves to the poached egg. Using a slotted spoon, gently remove the egg from the water. Serve immediately or, to reheat, gently lower the egg back into hot water with a slotted spoon for 1 to 2 minutes.

SOFT-SCRAMBLED

POACHED

Plain Omelet

Gently whisk 3 eggs with 2 tablespoons heavy cream in a bowl. Heat 1 tablespoon unsalted butter in a nonstick skillet over medium heat. Add the eggs and scramble, stirring constantly while tipping the pan so the uncooked eggs move around, until you have what looks like a soft-scrambled open-faced omelet with some uncooked portions, 45 seconds to 1 minute. Continue to cook, no longer stirring the eggs, for an additional minute. Tip the pan away from you and, using a silicone spatula, lift the edge of the omelet and gently fold one-third of it toward the center. Fold again in the same direction, tipping the pan once more to create the finished omelet. Gently slide the omelet onto a plate.

Filled Omelet

Follow the recipe for a plain omelet, stopping before you fold the omelet. Layer fillings such as sautéed mushrooms, goat cheese, and herbs about 2 inches from the center of the omelet on the side closer to you in a straight line, leaving an inch on each end of the omelet. Continue to cook for an additional minute. Tip the pan away from you and, using a silicone spatula, lift the edge of the omelet and gently fold one-third of it toward the center. Fold again, tipping the pan once more to create the finished omelet. Gently slide the omelet onto a plate and garnish with extra herbs.

PLAIN OMELET

FILLED OMELET

Sunny-Side Up

For each egg, heat 2 teaspoons each vegetable oil and unsalted butter in a nonstick skillet over medium-high heat. Make an initial, hearty crack of an egg on a flat surface (don't crack on the side of the skillet, which increases your chances of getting shells in the eggs), then crack the egg open over the skillet. Cook, basting the white occasionally with some of the hot fat, until the white is opaque and the edges are lacy and browned but the yolk is still shiny, 3 minutes. Slide the egg onto a plate and season with salt and pepper.

Over-Easy

Follow the steps for a sunny-side-up egg, then flip the egg and cook an additional 15 to 20 seconds. Slide onto a plate.

GOOD EGGS

WHEN SELECTING EGGS, look for those labeled "free-range" or "pasture-raised." Also, seek out eggs from your local farmer's market, which are more likely to be fresher, with sunny, golden-yellow yolks. (The fresher the better; older eggs can have runny, thin whites and yolks that have lost some of their creamy richness.)

SUNNY-SIDE UP

OVER-EASY

ACKNOWLEDGMENTS

To **ADEENA SUSSMAN**, *the best coauthor and recipe developer one could ever hope for. Thank you for your skillful eye and meticulous attention to detail, and for having the patience to deal with both the process and me for all these years.*

To the incomparable **EVAN SUNG**, *your work elevates every page of this book and every project you take on. More than a photographer, you are a true collaborator.*

To **KIMPTON HOTELS**, *thank you for housing us in style on so many stops along the way.*

To **JETBLUE AIRLINES** *and my travel agent extra-ordinaire,* **CAROL PRESS**, *for your assistance with air travel.*

To **MICHELLE MINYARD** *for always being our New Orleans go-to gal.*

To **EDMUND TIJERINA, JENNIFER MCINNIS, LAUREN CHARLIP**, *and* **PENNY DE LOS SANTOS** *for your help with the Texas trips; to* **LAUREN RAVITZ** *for your help with Los Angeles; to* **KATY DARNABY** *for your help with Chicago. To* **JENNIFER COLE** *and* **ANNETTE THOMPSON** *for help with Birmingham. To* **LEAH BHAHBA** *for your research talents.*

To **ANAT ABRAMOV SHIMONI** *for your invaluable help with recipe testing and organization; thank you as always!*

To the **FOOD NETWORK** *and* **COOKING CHANNEL SOUTH BEACH** *and* **NEW YORK CITY WINE & FOOD FESTIVAL TEAMS** *and* **SPECIAL EVENTS DEPARTMENT** *at* **SOUTHERN WINE & SPIRITS OF AMERICA**. *I simply couldn't do what I do without your unwavering support and dedication.*

To **LINDA DARNELL**, *my home economics teacher at Nova High School, for insisting that I put on an apron instead of going to woodshop class.*

To **WILL SCHWALBE** *for your constant and invaluable guidance, as ever.*

To **LISA QUEEN** *(Lee) and* **SHARON BOWERS** *(Adeena) for your fantastic agenting.*

To **AARON WEHNER, KATE TYLER, DORIS COOPER, ANGELIN BORSICS**, *and everyone at Clarkson Potter, thank you for supporting us on book #2.*

To **PAM KRAUSS** *for introducing me to the glorious world of cookbook writing, and for remaining in my corner ever since.*

C. J. TROPP, *thank you for your ruthless organizational skills, among countless other attributes.*

To my **MOM, DAD**, *and* **BROTHERS, RICHARD** *and* **HOWARD**, *for all of those wonderful breakfast memories at the Seaford Diner.*

To the **BROWNS**, *who truly make it all worthwhile.*

A

Aïoli
Malt, 110–12
Tomato, 215–16, *216*
Almonds
Roasted Potato Phyllo Pie, 218–20, *219*
Romesco Sauce, 218–20, *219*
Apples
Fruit Crepes with Whipped Crème Fraîche, *72*, *73*–74
Morning Glory Muffins, 160–63, *161*
Avocado(es)
The BLT Deluxe, 110–12, *111*
Chalupa Robert, 141–42, *143*
The Devil's Mess, 212–14, *213*
selecting, 112
Toast with Pickled Red Onions and Poached Eggs, 30, *31*

B

Bacon
The BLT Deluxe, 110–12, *111*
Breakfast Pizza, 20–22, *21*
Cheddar Potato Pancakes, 91
Egg, and Cheese "Paco," 154, *155*
Fennel-Maple Glazed, Breakfast Pang with, 193–95, *194*
Kimchi Brussels Sprouts, and Eggs, 208–9, *209*
Marlene Schrager's German Breakfast, 152, *153*
Oeufs en Meurette on Celery Root Rösti, 190–92, *191*
Bananas
Cannoli French Toast, 202–4, *203*
Barbecued Brisket Breakfast Burrito, 117, *117*
Basil
Pesto, 48, 103
Sugar, Caramelized Grapefruit with, *52*, *53*
sugar, serving ideas, 53
Beans
Chalupa Robert, 141–42, *143*
Puntillitas Salteadas, 225, *225*

White, Roasted Tomatoes, and Olives, Oven-Baked Eggs with, 24–27, *25*
Beef
Barbecued Brisket Breakfast Burrito, 117, *117*
The Big Hot Mess, 215–17, *216*
Chalupa Robert, 141–42, *143*
Chicken-Fried Steak, 69–70, *71*
Filipino Steak with Garlic Fried Rice, 94–95, *96*
Frito Pie, 148–50, *149*
Koko Moco, 56, *57*–59
Migas Tacos, 144–46, *145*
Noodle Soup (Pho Bo), 135–37, *136*
The Big Hot Mess, 215–17, *216*
Biscuits
Cheesy, and Vegetarian Gravy, 66–68, *67*
with Country Ham and Redeye Gravy, *138*, 139–40
Spelt, with Goat Cheese, Pecans, and Honey, 120, *121*
Bloody marys, favorite, 228–29, *228–29*
Blueberry(ies)
and Cheese Danish with Brown Butter Streusel, 98–101, *99*
Coconut Pancakes, *196*, 197
-Lemon Waffles, 85–86, *87*
Summer Granola, 180, *181*
Bread(s). *See also* Biscuits; Tortillas
Avocado Toast with Pickled Red Onions and Poached Eggs, 30, *31*
Brioche Cinnamon Buns, 122–25, *123*
Cannoli French Toast, 202–4, *203*
Cuban, Torrejas with Guava Syrup, Cream Cheese, and Maria Cookie Sugar, 164–66, *165*
Morning Glory Muffins, 160–63, *161*
Pretzel Croissant French Toast with Two Sauces, 76, *77*
Yemenite Fried (Malawach), 167–69, *168*
Yuca Buns, 170, *172*
Breakfasts: The Midwest
Chicago, IL, 91, 93, 94, 98, 102, 104, 229
Cleveland, OH, 82, 85, 88

Kansas City, MO, 73, 104
Minneapolis, MN, 75, 104
Omaha, NE, 66, 69
St. Louis, MO, 76, 78, 79, 229
Breakfasts: Northeast and Mid-Atlantic
Baltimore, MD, 208, 210, 211, 229
Brooklyn, NY, 198, 226
Cambridge, MA, 180
New York, NY, 183, 187, 189, 190, 193, 197, 226, 229
Philadelphia, PA, 201, 202, 205, 226
Richmond, VA, 212, 215
Washington, DC, 218, 221, 224, 225, 226, 229
Breakfasts: The South
Austin, TX, 144, 148
Birmingham, AL, 120, 174
Charleston, SC, 115
Houston, TX, 139
Memphis, TN, 117, 118
Miami, FL, 153, 154, 157, 159, 160, 164, 167, 170, 174, 229
New Orleans, LA, 128, 132, 135, 174, 229
Oxford, MS, 122, 127
Raleigh, NC, 110, 113
San Antonio, TX, 141
Breakfasts: West Coast and Pacific Northwest
Honolulu, HI, 57
Los Angeles, CA, 16, 19, 20, 24, 229
Los Angeles, Ca, 60
Portland, OR, 46, 49, 53, 54, 60, 229
San Francisco, CA, 29, 30, 33, 35, 37, 38, 43, 60
Brioche Cinnamon Buns, 122–25, *123*
Brussels Sprouts, Kimchi, Bacon, and Eggs, 208–9, *209*
Buns
Brioche Cinnamon, 122–25, *123*
Yuca, 170, *172*
Burrito, Barbecued Brisket Breakfast, 117, *117*
Butter, clarifying, 212

C

Cake Donuts, 200, *201*

Calas Cakes, 132–34, 133
Cannoli French Toast, 202–4, 203
Caramel Sauce, 76
Carrots
    Market Vegetable Omelet with Goat
        Cheese and Pesto, 102–3
    Morning Glory Muffins, 160–63, 161
Celery Root Rösti, Oeufs en Meurette on,
    190–92, 191
Chalupa Robert, 141–42, 143
Cháo (Vietnamese Chicken and Rice
    Porridge), 38–40, 39
Cheese
    Bacon, and Egg "Paco," 154, 155
    Bacon Cheddar Potato Pancakes, 91
    Barbecued Brisket Breakfast Burrito, 117, 117
    The Big Hot Mess, 215–17, 216
    and Blueberry Danish with Brown Butter
        Streusel, 98–101, 99
    Breakfast Pizza, 20–22, 21
    Cannoli French Toast, 202–4, 203
    Chalupa Robert, 141–42, 143
    Cheesy Biscuits and Vegetarian Gravy,
        66–68, 67
    Cream, Guava Syrup, and Maria Cookie
        Sugar, Cuban Bread Torrejas with, 164–66,
        165
    Croque Monsieur Sandwiches, 32, 33
    The Devil's Mess, 212–14, 213
    The Forager Sandwich, 205–6, 207
    Frito Pie, 148–50, 149
    Frittata with Seasonal Greens, 198, 199
    Goat, and Pesto, Market Vegetable Omelet
        with, 102–3
    Goat, Pecans, and Honey, Spelt Biscuits
        with, 120, 121
    Malawach (Yemenite Fried Bread), 167–69,
        168
    Migas Tacos, 144–46, 145
    Pesto, 48
    Queso, 150
    Quiche Lorraine, 158, 159
    Shrimp and Grits, 114, 115–16
    Southwestern Skillet, 126, 127
    The Yolko Ono Sandwich, 46–48, 47
Chicken
    Creole File Gumbo, 128–31, 129
    Fried, & Waffles, 221–22, 223

and Rice Porridge, Vietnamese (Cháo),
    38–40, 39
    Scrapple, 224, 224
    Southwestern Skillet, 126, 127
Chicken-Fried Steak, 69–70, 71
Chili Yogurt, 195
Chinese Doughnuts, 41–42, 42
Chocolate
    Cannoli French Toast, 202–4, 203
    Doughnuts and Crème Anglaise, 49–50, 51
    Nutella Sauce, 88–90, 89
    White, Sauce, 76
Cinnamon Buns, Brioche, 122–25, 123
Clams
    and Crab, Breakfast Spaghetti with, 92, 93
    removing meat from shells, 93
Coconut
    Morning Glory Muffins, 160–63, 161
    Pancakes, 196, 197
    Summer Granola, 180, 181
Corn
    and Andouille Skillet Fritters, 82–84, 83
    Southwestern Skillet, 126, 127
Crab
    Cakes with Homemade Tartar Sauce and
        Sunny Side Up Eggs, 225
    and Clams, Breakfast Spaghetti with, 92, 93
    Creole File Gumbo, 128–31, 129
Crème Anglaise, 49, 51
Crème Fraîche, Whipped, Fruit Crepes with,
    72, 73–74
Creole File Gumbo, 128–31, 129
Crepes, Fruit, with Whipped Crème Fraîche,
    72, 73–74
Croque Monsieur Sandwiches, 32, 33
Cuban Bread Torrejas with Guava Syrup,
    Cream Cheese, and Maria Cookie Sugar,
    164–66, 165

D

Danish, Blueberry and Cheese, with Brown
    Butter Streusel, 98–101, 99
The Devil's Mess, 212–14, 213
Dips and sauces
    Caramel Sauce, 76
    Chili Yogurt, 195
    Crème Anglaise, 49, 51
    Dona Sauce, 147

Hollandaise, 82
Malt Aïoli, 110–12
Mushroom Gravy, 59
Nutella Sauce, 88–90, 89
Pesto, 48, 103
Queso, 150
Romesco Sauce, 218–20, 219
Salsa Roja, 147
Tartar Sauce, 211
Tomato Aïoli, 215–17, 216
White Chocolate Sauce, 76
Doughnuts
    Cake Donuts, 200, 201
    Chinese, 41–42, 42
    Chocolate, and Crème Anglaise, 49–50, 51
Drinks
    favorite bloody marys, 228–29, 228–29
    Golden Turmeric Iced Latte, 16, 16
    Old-Fashioned Oatmeal (Avena) Breakfast
        Smoothies, 171, 171
    Strawberry Milkshake, 70, 71

E

Egg(s)
    Bacon, and Cheese "Paco," 154, 155
    Barbecued Brisket Breakfast Burrito, 117, 117
    The Big Hot Mess, 215–17, 216
    Biscuits with Country Ham and Redeye
        Gravy, 138, 139–40
    Breakfast Pang with Fennel-Maple Glazed
        Bacon, 193–95, 194
    Breakfast Pizza, 20–22, 21
    Breakfast Spaghetti with Clams and Crab,
        92, 93
    Chalupa Robert, 141–42, 143
    Cheesy Biscuits and Vegetarian Gravy,
        66–68, 67
    Chicken-Fried Steak, 69–70, 71
    Corn and Andouille Skillet Fritters, 82–84,
        83
    The Devil's Mess, 212–14, 213
    Farmer's Market Shakshuka, 186, 187–88
    Filipino Steak with Garlic Fried Rice, 94–95,
        96
    filled omelet, 232, 232
    The Forager Sandwich, 205–6, 207
    Frito Pie, 148–50, 149
    Frittata with Seasonal Greens, 198, 199

Kimchi Brussels Sprouts, and Bacon, 208–9, 209

Kimchi Pancakes, 54, 55

Koko Moco, 56, 57–59

Lobster Scrambled, 18, 19

Malawach (Yemenite Fried Bread), 167–69, 168

Market Vegetable Omelet with Goat Cheese and Pesto, 102–3

Marlene Schrager's German Breakfast, 152, 153

Migas Tacos, 144–46, 145

Oeufs en Meurette on Celery Root Rösti, 190–92, 191

Oven-Baked, with White Beans, Roasted Tomatoes, and Olives, 24–27, 25

over-easy, 233, 233

plain omelet, 232, 232

poached, 231, 231

Poached, and Pickled Red Onions, Avocado Toast with, 30, 31

Roasted Potato Phyllo Pie, 218–20, 219

selecting, 233

soft-scrambled, 231, 231

Soft-Scrambled, Hubbard Squash Puree with, 28, 29

Southwestern Skillet, 126, 127

sunny-side up, 233, 233

Sunny Side Up, and Homemade Tartar Sauce, Crab Cakes with, 211

Tortilla de Papas (Potato Omelet), 156, 157

The Yolko Ono Sandwich, 46–48, 47

F

Fennel-Maple Glazed Bacon, Breakfast Pang with, 193–95, 194

Filipino Steak with Garlic Fried Rice, 94–95, 96

French Toast

Cannoli, 202–4, 203

Pretzel Croissant, with Two Sauces, 76, 77

Frito Pie, 148–50, 149

Frittata with Seasonal Greens, 198, 199

Fritters

Calas Cakes, 132–34, 133

Corn and Andouille Skillet, 82–84, 83

Fruit. *See also specific fruits*

Baked Oatmeal with Raspberry Compote and Candied Pecans, 79–81, 80

Crepes with Whipped Crème Fraîche, 72, 73–74

Tart "Pop Tarts," 43–45, 44

G

Garlic

Fried Rice, Filipino Steak with, 94–95, 96

roasting, 223

German Breakfast, Marlene Schrager's, 152, 153

Graham Cracker Waffles, 88–90, 89

Grains. *See* Grits; Oats; Rice

Granola, Summer, 180, 181

Grapefruit, Caramelized, with Basil Sugar, 52, 53

Gravy

Mushroom, 59

Redeye, 138, 139

Greens. *See also* Kale

The BLT Deluxe, 110–12, 111

Farmer's Market Shakshuka, 186, 187–88

Seasonal, Frittata with, 198, 199

Grits, Shrimp and, 114, 115–16

Guava Syrup, Cream Cheese, and Maria Cookie Sugar, Cuban Bread Torrejas with, 164–66, 165

Gumbo, Creole File, 128–31, 129

H

Ham

Country, and Redeye Gravy, Biscuits with, 138, 139–40

Creole File Gumbo, 128–31, 129

Croque Monsieur Sandwiches, 32, 33

Hock Stock, 140

Quiche Lorraine, 158, 159

Hash Browns, 210

Hominy and Pork Stew (Pozole), 36, 37

K

Kale

The Forager Sandwich, 205–6, 207

Oven-Baked Eggs with White Beans, Roasted Tomatoes, and Olives, 24–27, 25

Kimchi

Brussels Sprouts, Bacon, and Eggs, 208–9, 209

Pancakes, 54, 55

Koko Moco, 56, 57–59

L

Latkes, Potato, with Toppings, 182, 183–84

Lemon-Blueberry Waffles, 85–86, 87

Lobster Scrambled Eggs, 18, 19

M

Malawach (Yemenite Fried Bread), 167–69, 168

Malt Aïoli, 110–12

Marshmallows

Graham Cracker Waffles, 88–90, 89

Migas Tacos, 144–46, 145

Milk

Old-Fashioned Oatmeal (Avena) Breakfast Smoothies, 171, 171

Strawberry Milkshake, 70, 71

Muffins, Morning Glory, 160–63, 161

Mushroom(s)

Cheesy Biscuits and Vegetarian Gravy, 66–68, 67

The Forager Sandwich, 205–6, 207

Gravy, 59

Koko Moco, 56, 57–59

Oeufs en Meurette on Celery Root Rösti, 190–92, 191

Shrimp and Grits, 114, 115–16

trumpet, about, 206

N

Nutella Sauce, 88–90, 89

Nuts

Baked Oatmeal with Raspberry Compote and Candied Pecans, 79–81, 80

Cannoli French Toast, 202–4, 203

Morning Glory Muffins, 160–63, 161

Roasted Potato Phyllo Pie, 218–20, 219

Romesco Sauce, 218–20, 219

Spelt Biscuits with Goat Cheese, Pecans, and Honey, 120, 121

O

Oats

Baked Oatmeal with Raspberry Compote and Candied Pecans, 79–81, 80

Old-Fashioned Oatmeal (Avena) Breakfast

Smoothies, 171, *171*
Summer Granola, 180, *181*
Olives, White Beans, and Roasted Tomatoes,
Oven-Baked Eggs with, 24–27, *25*
Omelets
filled, preparing, 232, *232*
Market Vegetable, with Goat Cheese and
Pesto, 102–3
plain, preparing, 232, *232*
Potato (Tortilla de Papas), 156, *157*
Onions
Marlene Schrager's German Breakfast,
152, *153*
Pickled Red, and Poached Eggs, Avocado
Toast with, 30, *31*

P

Pancakes
Bacon, Egg, and Cheese "Paco," 154, *155*
Bacon Cheddar Potato, 91
Coconut, 196, *197*
Kimchi, 54, *55*
Pasta and noodles
Breakfast Spaghetti with Clams and Crab,
92, *93*
Pho Bo (Beef Noodle Soup), 135–37, *136*
Pears
Fruit Crepes with Whipped Crème Fraîche,
72, *73–74*
Pecans
Candied, and Raspberry Compote, Baked
Oatmeal with, 79–81, *80*
Goat Cheese, and Honey, Spelt Biscuits
with, 120, *121*
Peppers
Chalupa Robert, 141–42, *143*
The Devil's Mess, 212–14, *213*
Dona Sauce, 147
Farmer's Market Shakshuka, *186*, 187–88
Malawach (Yemenite Fried Bread), 167–69,
168
Marlene Schrager's German Breakfast,
152, *153*
Romesco Sauce, 218–20, *219*
Salsa Roja, 147
Southwestern Skillet, 126, *127*
Pesto, 48, 103
Pho Bo (Beef Noodle Soup), 135–37, *136*

Pies
Frito, 148–50, *149*
Roasted Potato Phyllo, 218–20, *219*
Pineapple
Morning Glory Muffins, 160–63, *161*
Pizza, Breakfast, 20–22, *21*
Pizza Dough, 23
"Pop Tarts," Fruit Tart, 43–45, *44*
Pork. See also Bacon; Ham; Sausages
and Hominy Stew (Pozole), 36, *37*
Scrapple, 224, *224*
The Yolko Ono Sandwich, 46–48, *47*
Potato(es)
American Fries, 70, *71*
Barbecued Brisket Breakfast Burrito, 117, *117*
The Big Hot Mess, 215–17, *216*
Breakfast Pizza, 20–22, *21*
Chalupa Robert, 141–42, *143*
Chocolate Doughnuts and Crème Anglaise,
49–50, *51*
Hash Browns, 210
Latkes with Toppings, 182, *183–84*
Marlene Schrager's German Breakfast,
152, *153*
Omelet (Tortilla de Papas), 156, *157*
Pancakes, Bacon Cheddar, 91
Roasted, Phyllo Pie, 218–20, *219*
Southwestern Skillet, 126, *127*
Pozole (Pork and Hominy Stew), 36, *37*
Pretzel Croissant French Toast with Two
Sauces, 76, *77*
Puntillitas Salteadas, 225, *225*

Q

Queso, 150
Quiche Lorraine, 158, *159*

R

Raspberry Compote and Candied Pecans,
Baked Oatmeal with, 79–81, *80*
Rice
Calas Cakes, 132–34, *133*
Garlic Fried, Filipino Steak with, 94–95, *96*
Koko Moco, 56, *57–59*
Porridge and Chicken, Vietnamese (Cháo),
38–40, *39*
Rösti, Celery Root, Oeufs en Meurette on,
190–92, *191*

S

Salsa Roja, 147
Sandwiches
The BLT Deluxe, 110–12, *111*
Breakfast Pang with Fennel-Maple Glazed
Bacon, 193–95, *194*
Croque Monsieur, 32, *33*
The Forager, 205–6, *207*
The Yolko Ono, 46–48, *47*
Sauces. *See* Dips and sauces
Sausages
Corn and Andouille Skillet Fritters, 82–84,
83
Creole File Gumbo, 128–31, *129*
The Devil's Mess, 212–14, *213*
The Yolko Ono Sandwich, 46–48, *47*
Scrapple, 224, *224*
Shakshuka, Farmer's Market, *186*, 187–88
Shellfish
Breakfast Spaghetti with Clams and Crab,
92, *93*
Crab Cakes with Homemade Tartar Sauce
and Sunny Side Up Eggs, 211
Creole File Gumbo, 128–31, *129*
Lobster Scrambled Eggs, 18, *19*
Puntillitas Salteadas, 225, *225*
removing clam meat from shells, 93
Shrimp and Grits, 114, *115–16*
Shrimp
Creole File Gumbo, 128–31, *129*
and Grits, 114, *115–16*
Soups and stews
Creole File Gumbo, 128–31, *129*
Pho Bo (Beef Noodle Soup), 135–37, *136*
Pozole (Pork and Hominy Stew), 36, *37*
Spelt Biscuits with Goat Cheese, Pecans, and
Honey, 120, *121*
Squash
Hubbard, Puree and Soft-Scrambled Eggs,
28, *29*
Market Vegetable Omelet with Goat
Cheese and Pesto, 102–3
Squid
Puntillitas Salteadas, 225, *225*
Stock, Ham Hock, 140
Strawberry Milkshake, 70, *71*

T

Tacos
  Bacon, Egg, and Cheese "Paco," 154, 155
  Migas, 144–46, 145
Tart, Fruit, "Pop Tarts," 43–45, 44
Tartar Sauce, 211
Tomato(es)
  Aïoli, 215–17, 216
  The BLT Deluxe, 110–12, 111
  Chalupa Robert, 141–42, 143
  The Devil's Mess, 212–14, 213
  Farmer's Market Shakshuka, 186, 187–88
  Frito Pie, 148–50, 149
  Malawach (Yemenite Fried Bread), 167–69, 168
  Roasted, White Beans, and Olives, Oven-Baked Eggs with, 24–27, 25
  Salsa Roja, 147
Torrejas, Cuban Bread, with Guava Syrup, Cream Cheese, and Maria Cookie Sugar, 164–66, 165
Tortilla de Papas (Potato Omelet), 156, 157
Tortillas
  Barbecued Brisket Breakfast Burrito, 117, 117
  Chalupa Robert, 141–42, 143
  Migas Tacos, 144–46, 145
  Southwestern Skillet, 126, 127
Turmeric
  fresh, juicing, 16
  Iced Latte, Golden, 16, 16

V

Vegetable. See also specific vegetables
  Market, Omelet with Goat Cheese and Pesto, 102–3
Vietnamese Chicken and Rice Porridge (Cháo), 38–40, 39

W

Waffles
  & Fried Chicken, 221–22, 223
  Graham Cracker, 88–90, 89
  Lemon-Blueberry, 85–86, 87
White Chocolate Sauce, 76

Y

Yemenite Fried Bread (Malawach), 167–69, 168

Yogurt
  Chili, 195
  Roasted Potato Phyllo Pie, 218–20, 219
Yuca Buns, 170, 172

Z

Zucchini
  Market Vegetable Omelet with Goat Cheese and Pesto, 102–3